———— CONGREGATIONS & ————
CHURCH AGENCIES IN RELATIONSHIP

For I Was Hungry

──── EDITED BY JOHN G. FLETT ────

Published in Australia by
Uniting Academic Press
an imprint of Coventry Press
33 Scoresby Road
Bayswater VIC 3153

ISBN 9781922589194

Compilation Copyright © John G. Flett 2022
Copyright of individual chapters remains with the authors

All rights reserved. Other than for the purposes and subject to the conditions prescribed under the *Copyright Act*, no part of this publication may be reproduced, stored in a retrieval system, or transmitted in any form or by any means, electronic, mechanical, photocopying, recording or otherwise, without the prior permission of the publisher.

Catalogue-in-Publication entry is available from the National Library of Australia http://catalogue.nla.gov.au

Cover design by Ian James – www.jgd.com.au
Text design by Coventry Press
Set in Tex Gyre Pagella

Printed in Australia

Table of Contents

About the Contributors 5

Acknowledgments 9

1. Introduction: Differentiation, the Secularised Church, and Mission
   John. G. Flett 11

2. Inasmuch: Churches and Welfare in Australia; A Background History
   Shurlee Swain 28

3. Diaconal Action on the Basis of Christian Spirituality
   Johannes Eurich 44

4. Agencies and Congregations: Who Is the "Other" in Our Relationship and Why?
   Lucy Morris 63

5. Re-Membering the Body: Six Theses on Congregation, Church Agencies, and the Ecclesia of God
   Stephen Pickard 82

6. Beyond Religious Congregations and Secular Welfare: An Experiment in Uniting Church Ecclesiology
   Geoff Thompson 101

7. Towards a Theology of Social Service: A Reflection Paper after the UnitingCare Australia Leaders Forum
   Ji Zhang 张骥 124

8. Communicating the Gospel in Plural Places: Theology, Church Theory, and the Sociological Aspects of Contemporary Church Practice
   Annette Noller 158

9. Does Theology Matter? Or How Church-Related Agencies Can Become (or Not) an Extension of the State
   Douglas Hynd 177

10. Examining Mission Threat in a World of Competitive Tendering: Disability Employment Case Study
    Brendan Long 203

11. Together We Stand: The Need for the Church to Unite in the Face of Marketisation of Human Services
    Mark Zirnsak 234

About the Contributors

Johannes Eurich, extraordinary professor for practical theology at Stellenbosch University, Stellenbosch, South Africa, chair for practical theology and diaconal studies at Heidelberg University, Germany, was from 2013 to 2015 dean of the Theological Faculty at Heidelberg University. He serves on the board of national and international diaconal organisations and is member of the editorial board of the international journal *Diaconia*. In 2018, he was appointed chair of the international advisory board of VID Specialized University in Oslo, Norway.

John Flett is professor of missiology and intercultural theology at Pilgrim Theological College, University of Divinity. His main area of study concerns the theologies of mission which inform public and political action and community formation.

Douglas Hynd has worked in social policy, program management, and public sector reform in the public service and taught on church and society at St Marks National Theological Centre. He has undertaken a theologically informed inquiry into the impact of contracting with government on church-related social welfare agencies' mission and identity and is an adjunct research fellow at the Australian Centre for Christianity and Culture, Charles Sturt University. Doug is also president of Canberra Refugee Support providing community support and advocacy for refugees and asylum seekers in Canberra.

Brendan Long is an economist and religious academic with over two decades of experience in key government agencies (Treasury, Productivity Commission, the Department of Prime

Minister and Cabinet, and the Office of National Assessments) and has held leadership policy roles in national peak organisations in the private and not-for-profit sectors (including Catholic Social Services Australia and National Disability Services). He has also been a senior political adviser to federal politicians, including Simon Crean, Joel Fitzgibbon, Joseph Ludwig, and Stephen Conroy. His current academic role is Senior Research Fellow, Australian Centre for Christianity and Culture, Charles Sturt University.

Lucy Morris is an ordained Anglican priest (2014) who held leadership positions in WA's community sector, including as Baptistcare WA's CEO for 8 years. Previously she worked in drugs and alcohol services for the NHS, and as a journalist in the UK. Lucy has a BA Hons 1st Class degree and an M.Phil in theology from Manchester University. Her PhD from Curtin University WA researched "leadership, ethics, values and spirituality in NGOs and the integration of personal and organisational belief systems." She is now a parish priest in the Anglican Diocese of Bunbury.

Annette Noller was professor of theology and in social ethics/diaconal studies at the University of Applied Sciences in Ludwigsburg, Germany (2002-2020). She worked for several years in the Federal Association of Diakonie in Germany. One of her main projects was the cooperation of diaconal agencies with parishes and especially the communication and implementation of diaconal profile in the Federal German Association of Diakonie. She was the vice chair of the board of a local diaconal agency (Evangelische Gesellschaft Stuttgart—EVA) with about 1,500 employees. Since 2020, she has served as chair of the board of directors of the regional diaconal Association in Württemberg which bears responsibility for with 1400 diaconal agencies. She is a member of the conference of Diakonie Deutschland.

Stephen Pickard is an adjunct professor at Charles Sturt University and former executive director of the Australian Centre for Christianity and Culture. Until his retirement in 2002, he was an assistant bishop in the Anglican Diocese of Canberra and Goulburn and chair of its Public Issues Commission. He has served in a range of ministerial and academic appointments over three decades in Australia and the United Kingdom. He was acting CEO of Anglicare Canberra Goulburn from 2012 to 2013. His teaching and writing interests are in church, culture, mission, interfaith and science/theology dialogue. He was a former chair of the Mission and Ministry Commission of the Anglican Church of Australia, and member of the Doctrine Commission. He served over two decades on the Archbishop of Canterbury's theological, doctrinal and ecumenical international commissions.

Shurlee Swain is an emeritus professor at Australian Catholic University and a fellow of the Academy of the Humanities and Academy of the Social Sciences. As a social historian, she has focused her work on the interaction of women and children with the welfare system and has informed several of the recent Australian inquiries into historical institutional abuse.

Geoff Thompson is associate professor of systematic theology at Pilgrim Theological College, University of Divinity. His writing on the Uniting Church's theology includes *Disturbing Much, Disturbing Many: Theology Provoked by the Basis of Union* (Northcote: UAP, 2016) and *A Genuinely Theological Church: Ministry, Theology and the Uniting Church* (Northcote: UAP, 2018). On broader issues his most recent publication is *Christian Doctrine: A Guide for the Perplexed* (London: T&T Clark, 2020).

Ji Zhang is the Assembly Theologian in Residence at the Uniting Church in Australia, National Assembly. Born in Shanghai, Ji has studied in Melbourne and Boston and has a PhD in comparative philosophy and theology. His postdoctoral research was published as *One and Many: A Comparative Study of Plato's Philosophy and Daoism Represented by Ge Hong*. Ji also works for UnitingCare Australia on theology of social service and coordinates the partnership with China Christian Council.

Mark Zirnsak is the Senior Social Justice Advocate of the Synod of Victoria and Tasmania, Uniting Church in Australia. Mark is a member of the Victorian Responsible Gambling Ministerial Advisory Council, the Commonwealth Government Open Government Forum, Alcohol Change Victoria, and the Secretariat for the Tax Justice Network in Australia. He is also active in anticorruption movements, including Transparency International Australia.

Acknowledgments

This text originated from a conference hosted both by Pilgrim Theological College, the Uniting Church synod of Victoria and Tasmania, the University of Divinity, and The Institute for the Study of Christian Social Service (DWI) of the University of Heidelberg, Germany. Anyone who has arranged a conference will know of all the work that occurs in the background. Special thanks is due to the Centre for Theology and Ministry and to Merryn Gray and Ann Byrne for administrative support, to Bret Salinger for the creative conference logo and accompanying art, and to my co-convener Bessy Andriotis. The question of the relationship between church agencies and the congregations can be one filled with tension, and this conference was a deliberate attempt to bring a diversity of voices and expertise into conversation. The success of the conference was due in large part to the good will and active participation of the various agencies of the Uniting Church in Australia but also those from other denominations. Peter McDonald was an engaged conversation partner throughout and so too were the leaders of Uniting from the synods of especially New South Wales and Queensland. There were many more presenters than could be included in this single text, including Hanns-Stephan Haas, Brian Howe, Heather den Houting, Jenny Tymms, Paul Oslington, Peter Worland, and Rick Morrell. Their experiences as theorists, policymakers, and administrators contributed to the richness of voice evident at the conference and spoke to many, varied, and creative resources at our disposal to identify and address the key questions. A further debt of thanks is due to Johannes Eurich

"For I was hungry…"

of Heidelberg University for his generosity and support and for his ongoing work with these important questions. It is impossible in a single conference to address the complexity of this key issue and to do so in a way that will satisfy the range of people wrestling with it, and so a final thank you is due to all the participants who contributed their questions, frustrations, and joys. The conference developed in the awareness of the different levels and types of discourses central to the question of the relationship between congregations and agencies. While this text reflects a more academic register, I hope that it contributes to a fuller and unfolding conversation. In this regard, a thank you also to Lauren Murphy for preventing many academic blushes through her editorial work.

John G. Flett

Introduction: Differentiation, the Secularised Church, and Mission

John G. Flett

The relationship between church agencies and the congregations out of which they grew is increasingly complex and even, on occasion, fraught.[1] While historically the churches often pointed to the provision of health services and education as part of their congregational mission, one sometimes today hears the argument that the ongoing mission of Jesus Christ is centred within the agencies and that the time of congregations is past. On the one hand, this reflects a contest of financial and property resources in a time of decline. On the other, far from a simple pragmatic concern, this is a matter of significant theological import and especially so during a period when the churches are dealing with questions of their own identity and forms of relating to their own social contexts. What effects accrue to social service provision when that is detached from a worshipping community? What is "Christian" about a professionalised agency, especially if key leaders have no ongoing relationship to a worshipping community? What consequences follow for a worshipping community should it hand its mission of service over to external agencies and direct its energies inwards to its own life?

---

[1] This is a substantially modified version of an article first published as "Differentiation, the Secularised Church and Mission," *Zadok Perspectives* 135 (2018): 14–15.

This common line of questioning is a negative one—it assumes a necessary decay in the relationship. While it is necessary to question this basic framing assumption, there are perhaps two main reasons for its existence: the first concerns the professionalisation, regulation, and changing funding models of social service provision; the second has to do with the processes of secularisation and the immediate consequences of these for the churches' forms of organisation and even self-understanding.

With regard to the professionalisation and regularisation of social service provision, there is an occasional sense that this shift represents a *fait accompli* against which local congregations have no voice. The primary need, by extension, is to educate the hosting institution (the church) as to its legal position, associated risks, and revised responsibilities in this changed context. But is this simply the case? Without question, each institution needs to comply with the legal and regulatory requirements. These, more often than not, exist for the safety of both the host institutions and the clients. But regulations change and do so in part due to conversation with stakeholder institutions. There is an evident way in which social services exist within a false economy: churches often provide a good deal of the base infrastructure for free or at low cost (property, volunteer or subsidised workers, etc). Compliance issues can include the drawing of church property more within the regulatory system of service provision, but this can also mean increasing costs which are then passed on to the churches due to this historic and false economy. Churches and congregations do not have to remain passive in this relationship; they can use the leverage available to them to be active in the relationship and so to confer a sense of their own identity and mission onto it. Of course, negotiations may break down and relationships end. While such endings might cause some pain, they can also be moments of opportunity: as one form of service provision perhaps grows beyond the capacities of a church body, it can be given its autonomy, and a smaller ministry which addresses another particular local need might develop in its place. The churches need not be passive in relation to either their own agencies or the state. Choices can be made that benefit the church's own understanding of its mission (including hiring policies, board memberships, educational opportunities) to inform in positive ways these historic and ongoing relationships.

A more significant force in directing social service provision is an underlying political and economic ideology which informs the value system and telos of social service itself. As one blatant example, in an interview with *Woman's Own*, Margret Thatcher is famous for stating: "There is no such thing [as society]! There are individual men and women and there are families and no government can do anything except through people and people look to themselves first."[2] When governments and the authors of public policy allow this position to inform budgets along with regulatory and legislative action, then a begrudging system of social services is an evident consequence, one directed by the assumption that individuals and families are not doing enough for themselves. It is only a short distance from this to motivate social services via a nexus of economics and profit. But a social service system that so lacks in grace, one for which "creaming and parking" is functionally the most "profitable" model, is not

---

[2] The text of the interview is available online at: https://www.margaretthatcher.org/document/106689.

the only or "best" one.³ It is possible to engage in a wider social and cultural discussion which decries this a proper end and so rejects the associated funding models (including models which set as a condition the prohibition of any negative commentary).

Compliance is important, but so is vision. Churches have the theological and social duty to imagine and embody different ways of seeing and working for the social good. No doubt this is a difficult task, and a good number of voices might frame a solution in terms of a return to past patterns of relationship in which the church had a more certain place within the social order. Much is to be cherished and remembered from this past, and these origin stories remain important in ongoing forms of education. Yet, any educational enterprise will require elements and approaches that encourage and enable critical praxis on the past, as well as introduction and enculturation into new ways of thinking about and the practices of these forms of faith in Christ. In seeking intentional ways of being together, ways that promote a mutual understanding of the mission directing both agencies and congregations, a clear need exists for a formal conversation concerning both the theological ground and its necessary community form, along with the professional and legal realities governing the agencies. A fractious and decaying relationship between congregations and agencies is not a given. The opposite is true: given that both are rooted in a shared witness to the mission of Jesus Christ, the relationship is to be mutually informing and life giving.

---

[3] Ian Greer, Lisa Schulte, and Graham Symon, "Creaming and Parking in Marketized Employment Services: An Anglo-German Comparison," *Human Relations* 71, no. 11 (2018): 1427–53.

A second concern informing the relationship of agencies and congregations is that of the processes of secularisation and the apparent loss of the churches' social standing and political authority in contemporary Western societies. Secularisation theory today takes three broad forms: classic secularisation, supply-side or rational-choice religious market, and individualisation. As an overly simplistic summary, "classic" secularisation theory treated religion as a sociocultural system which would lose ground as modernisation and rationalisation gained social significance. Secularisation, in this example, refers to the change in social structures and an associated decline in belief. "Supply side" theory charts the end of a religious monopoly and the rise of a competitive religious marketplace. Secularisation refers to the growth of religious pluralism and so the potential growth offered by choice. For "individualisation" theory, each person creates her or his own path to the ultimate and experiences this through eclectic spiritual events and workshops. Secularisation refers to the decline of communal forms of religious belonging. All three approaches offer important insight into the contemporary shape of the church and conceptions of its mission into and for the world.

The purpose of this brief summary in relation to the church-related welfare agencies is twofold. First, it highlights how the simple loss of belief plays a smaller part in the processes of secularisation. Second, it directs attention to the organisation of the social sphere and the form the church takes in response to its changing shape. The significance of this position for the church is thus: it is possible to retain a strong belief system *and* to become a secular institution. As strange as it may sound, the church is today itself a secular institution.[4] This secularisation of the institution frames the Western church's mission and identity as well as shaping its relationship to its own agencies. While it may well sound contentious to name worshipping communities as themselves secular bodies organised and directed within a secular view of the world, reference to the idea of "differentiation" and, more specifically, to that of "functional differentiation" helps illustrate the point.

The "differentiation" of social spheres is basic to the classic theory of secularisation. To cite José Casanova, secularisation is the "transfer of persons, things, meanings, etc., from ecclesiastical or religious to civil or lay use, possession, or control."[5] Whereas the church of Western Christendom influenced, to varying degrees, law, politics, economics, education, and health, contemporary societies *differentiate* these aspects of human society into separate spheres: for example, we today have a sphere of "education" with its own political head and its own understanding of its proper end. Each sphere becomes governed by its own best practices, oriented to its own end, and develops a professional class that theorises about this end and associated processes and that retains governing control.

Note, however, that as these spheres become independent entities, so too religion becomes an independent entity. It is itself differentiated into its own functional sphere and directed to a particular end, i.e., religion and spirituality.

Two important points follow: first, this process of functional differentiation separates the church from its historic connections in health, education, and politics. Given that much of the

---

[4] Jaco Beyers, "Self-Secularisation as Challenge to the Church," *HTS Teologiese Studies / Theological Studies* 71, no. 3 (2015): 1–10.

[5] José Casanova, "Rethinking Secularisation: A Global Comparative Perspective," *Hedgehog Review* 8 (2006): 7–22.

church's mission activity of the nineteenth and twentieth centuries centred on hospitals and schools, a good deal of anxiety attaches to the paths by which the church might today "connect" with the world. In even stronger terms: the old pathways by which the church related to the wider society are now, in part, defined by their distinction from the church. One might illustrate the point by reference to "Births, Deaths, and Marriages." Whereas the church in previous generations followed the course of an individual and family's life (baptism/christening, catechism, marriage, pastoral care, burial), today an individual has no need to reference the church or religion. Every major life event can be celebrated via a form within a government department. Religion has ceased to be a broad social program which assumed the allegiance of the wider social body. Where in the past individuals had to make a particular decision to "opt out" of the church and its social spheres, today individuals are assumed outside religious adherence until they "opt in." Where in the past the churches were naturally integrated into the social responsibilities of health and education, and in the pastoral contexts of prisons and service to the poor and socially marginal, today they need to make sustained arguments as to why these now distinguished spheres should include some religious element.

Nor, when it is invited into these spheres, does the church occupy a privileged position in relation to other religious bodies. There is a necessary pluralism of services regulated by competition and contractual obligations. This sets the church's traditional forms of mission within a market system. To put this in terms of social "rationalisation," within a religiously plural society the church must package and sell its "commodities." The economic language is here deliberate simply because the human relations in question tend to be contractual, organised, planned, and based on instrumental values. What one believes does not enter the discussion (except as a potential motivating factor).

Church agencies occupy, not in the first instance the religious sphere, but the one in which they conduct their main activities: education, health, social service. It means compliance with standards, regulations, and best practices internal to these spheres—including the distance from religion. With service standards becoming ever more professional and funding itself linked to this and the array of attached legislative standards, agencies will be further operationally distanced from the faith communities (liturgies, stories, practices, forms of gathering, external expressions, etc.) which may have birthed them.

The second important point concerns the sphere into which the church finds itself differentiated. The church has a religious social function. Or, given that this is religion defined in isolation from other social institutions, the proper activity of the church relates to "spirituality" and this as a form of salvation (its completion often includes the health and ecology narratives). This, at least, informs the expectation of what religion offers in its particular sphere: a secular definition of spirituality. And, insofar as this reflects a more general understanding, it often appears within the church as a potential avenue of connection with the wider social body and finds correspondence in what the church expects of itself. Emphasis falls on forms of spirituality and idiosyncratic liturgical formulations that often prove difficult to set in relationship to more robust social and political discourse. Within mainline churches, discussions of identity within this period of secularisation tend to turn to "the tradition" as itself echoing this limited secular account of spirituality and do so by trying to "recover" older rhythms of spiritual practice.

Though it delivers a religious service, however, as an ordered sphere within a technocratic society the church follows the patterns of governance, best practices, compliance, efficiency in management, and professionalisation common to all these spheres. Though it is possible to confuse this with traditional theological questions concerning ordination and the nature of the clergy/lay relationship, it speaks more to organisational patterns and standards of professionalism.

In many instances, evident benefits follow. Safe Church and the ongoing work of the Royal Commission into Institutional Responses to Child Sexual Abuse are clear examples. But this is not without its difficulties. The organisation itself conforms to its own secularisation with a professional class operating with no necessary reference to a living theological discourse but instead trained in managerial strategy, government compliance, legal statues of incorporation, media communications, and governance structures that mirror corporate efficiencies. While a theological voice may (or may not) inform the business of religion, it is unnecessary to these dominant secular forms of governance and the resulting management structures and "line reporting."

The more the church *de facto* confirms the rightness of this differentiated space (both in its assuming forms of governance driven by a CEO/CFO "product" model, budgets adverse to "human labour" costs, and accepting the rightness of the secular account of spirituality), the more tenuous the connections between it and its agencies, because the less influence there is of the theological over the operational aspects of either the church or its agencies. The oft-heard refrain that the agencies have become the key form of the church and of the mission of Jesus Christ indicates well the problem. It is important to observe, however, the identity of the forms of governance across these two spheres—religious and health services—created by the processes of differentiation and how these correspond to the secular mandate. One significant challenge for the church lies in how this concentration on governance directs its mission, i.e., restricts it to an internal spiritual mandate (in terms of its given responsibility under the conditions of differentiation), and thereby focuses the church's own externality in its agencies but without reference to the theological ground of this ministry in Jesus Christ and his body.

The above is a mere overview and fails to nuance the differences in how churches are structured or between the variety of agencies, but the main point should be clear: within Western societies, the church exists as a secular institution. Even while secularised, it can retain its religious function and own internal systems of belief. Indeed, it must retain its religious function because this is the role it plays within a secular society. But, in terms of its management, it structures itself according to the framing narrative of differentiation and corporation. One obvious point is that real theological challenges concerning the shape of the church today will not be solved by ever greater recourse to secular doctrine, especially one bearing all the hallmarks of neoliberalism.

A second observation concerns the dilapidated understanding of mission driving much of the discussion. Hospitals and schools were the primary forms of missionary outreach for a good deal of recent history. If the church no longer has this direct connection, what is its form of missionary outreach? Though not much attention is given to the question, the binary it forces on us is clear and corresponds to the structure of differentiation: congregations or service provision?

If this description of the problem corresponds in some way to the reality, then it suggests some clear responses centred on re-establishing connection. First, the legislative frameworks may well be good and needed, but they should also be developed in service to the mission of the church and its agencies. It is necessary to have a living theological discourse to inform the managerial considerations. One might think of this in terms of the same language surrounding "corporate culture." The culture and rhythms of the institution are to be shaped by the rhythms of faith, forgiveness, love, mercy, compassion, and at least some notional understanding of Jesus Christ and his mission. There is no need to be embarrassed by this, even within a secular society. A key element of this is to find people who are expert *both* in the legislative and organisational requirements *and* in theology. Hiring within agencies should include some reference to theological education or at least the intention to undertake such study. Big decisions concerning contracts and tendering require a guiding theological vision.

Second, we need robust cross-pollination between church bodies and agencies. Representation on boards or ministerial placements within agencies has often proven insufficient to retain a close relationship with church bodies. Where no "natural" relationship exists, then the manufacture of this becomes artificial and time- and energy-consuming. It is then a question of creating natural relationships, and this might be accomplished by sharing the same building, drawing local congregations into aspects of the service provision itself (where appropriate) or events by which agencies and congregations build personal relationships.

Third, the mission theology underlying this whole discussion requires sustained attention. We often use theological statements and mission principles, but the connection between these and the daily operation of both church and agency seems tenuous. Theology functions as a form of validation that does not really inform institutional shape and is reduced to sound bites and catchphrases. Nor is revisiting old patterns the best option. The church needs to think, make mistakes, and revise. There is freedom and joy in this process, along with witness and service.

Such is the purpose of this book. It is a deliberate attempt to place theological discourses beside the economic, policy, and governance realities of social service provision. It has no particular agenda apart from developing avenues for listening and learning. The contributors bring a range of experiences from holding positions of ecclesiastical authority to those with significant experience within government departments and leadership roles within agencies.

The first essay by Shurlee Swain is a historical study of the development of social service provision by the Christian churches from the early nineteenth and through the twentieth centuries within the Australian context. It begins with a significant change of direction from the "Poor Law" system then current in England to one of subscriber charities. Because the government was less represented on the committees, this created space for the churches. What follows is a story of the churches taking the lead in social service provision through to the middle of the twentieth century. It was only in the 1960s and in conjunction with the post–World War II professionalisation of welfare services that this arrangement of church and state began to fracture, and along with it the relationship between the churches and their agencies.

This direction intensified in the 1970s with changing models of financing (competitive tender) and with the government embracing a value system that church-based agencies saw as counter to their own values. Swain concludes that the contemporary relationship of the churches to the state is as simple competitors in an open market.

If questioning what makes a church-based agency "Christian" is one legacy of this history, the essay by Johannes Eurich argues for the ground of diaconal action in the doctrine of justification. God's unlimited love is bestowed on all humanity. Recognising this promotes a universal ethos of helping people in need, irrespective of religious, ethnic, or other differences. In this sense Protestant spirituality is oriented towards shaping the world through diaconal action. Eurich traces the significance of this single theological axiom for civil society, the ongoing meaning of social capital, and for Christian communities acting in their neighbourhoods.

Lucy Morris filters this same question of the theological ground and practice of social service provision through the idea of the "Other." The temptation in today's globalised, connected world is to accept the constraints and the definitions of "others" set by governments, business, and civil society. For agencies and congregations, however, resisting this postmodern, post-truth autonomous reality must be the starting point in seeking to understand God, our relationship with God, and God's creation. Seeing God as the "other" means we must take risks, do things differently, and work instead towards a relational future in a shared faithful community. This feeds directly, for Morris, into the question of "good governance" and to models which are moving away from "best practice" to relational and contingent approaches. It is not possible to set questions of financing, sustainability, and professionalism apart from the issue of the relationship between congregations and agencies—only in forms of governance which foster this relationship will these other issues find their place.

Stephen Pickard begins by observing the natural complexity of being the church in the world. One way of addressing this complexity has been to identify, differentiate, and develop particular dimensions of the church's life and witness. The strategy becomes problematic when the various sectors of the Body of Christ lose their connection with each other. Agencies can easily become seduced by external pressures and opportunities and forfeit their inner ecclesial identity. Congregations, shorn of the links which help orient them to the world, risk forfeiting their missional relevance. Pickard argues for a more integrative ecclesiology in which identity and relevance operate in reciprocal relation. By extension, agencies need to be seen as part of the ecclesial process itself and so are grounded in worship and mission, and the relationship between churches and agencies needs to be grounded in a common reaching to the kingdom of God. Drawing on John Chrysostom, this will involve a re-membering of the Body of Christ.

Geoff Thompson observes the degree to which the discourse about the future of church-based community-service agencies assumes as basic the categories of "secular" and "religion." He, however, rejects this distinction as anachronistic and ill-suited to the contemporary post-secular cultural and political circumstances of the church and its agencies. This leads to a critique of a recent position which considers the future of the Uniting Church in Australia in terms of "secular welfare," one which consists solely in the work of the agencies. Informed by the *Basis of Union*, the constructive argument moves towards a vision of both congregations and agencies adapting their respective self-understandings in the light of a post-secular reading of both congregations and agencies. Thompson seeks a theo-politics for a post-secular age in which Christian politics is of its very nature a perennial experiment and sees the ongoing question of the relationship of congregations and agencies as properly part of that experiment.

Ji Zhang attempts to develop a theology of social service. Beginning with the text "Faith Foundations," the guiding document for the theology of the Uniting Church in Australia (UCA) agency UnitingCare, Zhang notes that the theology has failed to keep up with the changing relationship between churches and service provision. This change is due both to a shift in the relationship between church and state and, as a result of this, a developing ecclesial problem—what is the nature and function of the church? Zhang turns to the theology of salvation assumed within this UCA documentation. After tracing certain inadequacies with this position (notably its tendency towards a monodirectional movement from church to world), and in conversation with Daoist insights, he develops a constructive theological account of a "service-church."

Annette Noller, reflecting on thirty years of sociological investigation into the church in Germany, observes one clear finding: in modern, differentiated societies, churches no longer assume one social shape but now develop plural forms of organisation. If church members are called to witness to the gospel to every member of society, the church should not rely on only one shape of organisation; it should look to an organisational plurality. Noller argues that parishes *and* diaconal agencies both develop church in different forms and engage in ways that are properly part of a multi-perspective church serving in a plurality of place.

Douglas Hynd examines the impact contracting with the government has had on church-related social welfare agencies in Australia over recent decades. Recent research has demonstrated that such contracting resulted in agencies becoming, at least partially, extensions of the state. To illustrate this, Hynd turns to the experience of the Salvation Army in contracting to provide offshore humanitarian services for asylum seekers and church-related agencies' experience with employment services. Such co-opting often occurred due to the agencies in question being unaware of the full significance of the policy it was involved in implementing. In the case of the Salvation Army and the detention of asylum seekers, its own mission and religious identity gave way to the underlying abusive policy logic of deterrence and detention. Hynd, however, does not view this outcome as inevitable. He argues for the power of theological commitments as fostering resistance to these contrary pressures.

Brendan Long, continuing this questioning of funding models, examines the problem of "mission drift": the idea that the original goal of an enterprise is captured by forces beyond its control to encompass wider concerns with a cost to the original objective. He argues that social service delivery has become constrained, and in some cases totally incapacitated, by the proscriptive nature of a government tendering model and extreme constraints of government regulatory requirements. Developing a case study from disability employment and drawing on Catholic Social Teaching (CST), Long indicates how agencies working within christological principles were more likely to take on clients with more challenging conditions and who were less likely to receive the same extended service from for-profit providers. Christian social services providers need to be able to interact with regulators to ensure not only that regulation and tendering models do no lead to mission drift but equally do not involve mission threat.

In the concluding chapter, Mark Zirnsak argues strongly for the need for the churches to collaborate in opposition to the marketisation of human services. For Zirnsak, human services in Australia face two significant threats. The first corresponds to the neoliberal agenda and the marketisation of every social sector, with human services being the latest target. Such an approach threatens the quality of service provision, especially as those delivering the services are forced into cutthroat competition with each other. The second threat lies in the neoliberal commitment to cut government revenue, reducing funding for human services as well as reducing the ability of governments to ensure the quality of services. The Uniting Church in Australia needs to respond by uniting its social justice and community service arms to continue to protect high-quality services that meet the needs of the people accessing them.

These essays reflect well the complexity surrounding the relationship between congregations and agencies. There is no one simple answer, but entering the conversation in a mutual spirit of service to the mission of Jesus Christ is the singular beginning point.

Inasmuch: Churches and Welfare in Australia; A Background History

Shurlee Swain

When nineteenth-century philanthropists sought to persuade churchgoers to contribute to their causes the most commonly invoked text was always Matthew 25:40: "Inasmuch as ye have done it unto one of the least of these my brethren, ye have done it unto me." This verse became so familiar that, in some contexts, it could be referred to simply as the "Inasmuch." Very neatly it reminded the potential giver that the poor stood in the place of Christ and that, therefore, in helping them they could provide direct service to the Lord. While religion and philanthropy are entwined in most Western societies, the historical conditions at the time of the British colonization of Australia have given this relationship a distinctive form. Religious organisations sponsored the earliest charitable provision in the colonies, and they continue to provide a large proportion of Australia's welfare services today. The role of this chapter is to explore the historical origins of this pattern of cooperation.

In the England from which the first immigrants arrived, the "Poor Law" guaranteed a minimal level of relief for widows and children, the infirm, the elderly, and the unemployed who were unable to provide for themselves. Funded by a tax on the ratepayers, the system struggled in the face of the Industrial Revolution and increasingly included harsh provisions designed to deter all but the most desperate from seeking relief. Voluntary charities provided a second level of assistance. These were founded by philanthropists and focused on rescuing the "deserving poor" from the degradation of the Poor Law workhouses. It was this second type of charity that appealed to Australia's early settlers. Although some assisted immigrants had direct experience of the Poor Law, most knew it only through the writing of influential critics and saw no place for such a harsh system in their new communities. As aspirational immigrants, they believed in the potential of the colonies and were unwilling to have their hoped-for wealth taxed in order to support those they saw as failing to take advantage of what the colonies had to offer.[1]

In the early convict settlements, the British government provided the basic services that sick or elderly convicts required. As the convict system declined and the strength of civil society increased, these institutions were reconstructed as voluntary charities. Supporters of new charitable initiatives often crafted their appeals for support by stressing the need to avoid the introduction of the hated poor laws, despite the fact that most such organisations were heavily dependent on government contributions.[2] Structured as subscriber charities, these organisations had no place on their committees of management for the governments which were often their largest single subscribers. It was this unique arrangement which created the space for the charitable work of the churches to expand and prosper.

---

[1] Brian Dickey, "Why Were There No Poor Laws in Australia?," *Journal of Policy History* 4, no. 2 (1992): 111–33.

[2] "To the Editor of the Sydney Monitor," *The Sydney Monitor*, 8 June 1833, 3, http://nla.gov.au/nla.news-article32143908; "Untitled," *The Australian*, 25 July 1837, 2, http://nla.gov.au/nla.news-article36854590.

Australia's first charitable institution, the Female Orphan School, opened in Sydney in 1801. It was funded by the New South Wales governor, Philip Gidley King, but was managed by a committee dominated by Anglican clergy. The hospitals that were transferred from the convict system, or established independently in nonconvict colonies, were broader in their reach, drawing their committees from clergy of all denominations rather than relying on the Anglicans alone.[3] Despite their determination to avoid a poor law, most colonies still developed generic institutions that looked and functioned very much like workhouses. Only in the struggling colony of Western Australia was the initial generic institution under direct government control.[4] In the other colonies, voluntary charities received varying amounts of government support but generally looked to regular churchgoers for their workforce and supporters. Sydney's Benevolent Asylum, which opened in 1821, had its origins in the New South Wales Society for Promoting Christian Knowledge, founded by the evangelical Christian Edward Smith Hall and his philanthropic friends in 1813.[5] Adelaide's Destitute Asylum, founded in 1851, was managed by the colony's Destitute Board, four of whose five members had church affiliations.[6] The Immigrants' Home which opened in Melbourne in 1853

---

[3] "Original Correspondence," *Melbourne Times*, 8 August 1843, 3, http://nla.gov.au/nla.news-article226924188.

[4] Penelope Hetherington, *Paupers, Poor Relief & Poor Houses in Western Australia 1829–1910* (Perth: University of Western Australia Press, 2009).

[5] Tanya Evans, *Fractured Families: Life on the Margins in Colonial New South Wales* (Sydney: NewSouth Publishing, 2015), 2–3.

[6] "Report of Destitute Board," *South Australian Register*, 19 January 1850, 4, http://nla.gov.au/nla.news-article38435744. James Farrell (Anglican), Michael Ryan (Roman Catholic), and Robert Haining (Presbyterian) were clergymen, while the businessman William Giles was a leading Congregationalist layman.

had its origins in the Immigrants' Aid Society with Protestant clergy making up half of its committee.[7] In Brisbane, the hospital, managed by a committee of clergy and laymen, accommodated the destitute.[8]

The existence of such generic institutions produced a pressure to separate out different groups believed to be deserving of better treatment than the poorhouses had to offer. The preference for voluntary action remained strong, but the cross-denominational committees of the earlier institutions proved harder to replicate. While the Church Act of 1836 removed any possibility of there being an established church in the colonies, it preserved a place for the churches in the emerging polity, collaborating with the state to frame a "social morality" and Christian citizenship.[9] Given the demographics of denominational affiliation and wealth distribution in the colonies, however, the community leaders who made up the committees of the new organisations tended to be Protestants who subscribed to a broad Evangelical Christianity. Protestants had an organisational as well as an economic advantage. Married clergy were able to depute much of the day-to-day management of institutions and the face-to-face contact with the poor to their wives and daughters. Catholic clergy, by contrast, had to spread themselves more thinly. The origins of many of these institutions lay with philanthropic women

---

[7] "The Stranger," *The Argus*, 13 May 1853, 6, http://nla.gov.au/nla.news-article4792570.

[8] "Domestic Intelligence," *The Moreton Bay Courier*, 17 January 1851, 2, http://nla.gov.au/nla.news-article3716352.

[9] Stuart Piggin, "Power and Religion in a Modern State: Desecularisation in Australian History," *Journal of Religious History* 38, no. 3 (2014): 320–40, here 328–29; David Stoneman, "Richard Bourke: For the Honour of God and the Good of Man," *Journal of Religious History* 38, no. 3 (2014): 341–55, here 342.

who came together to relieve the need they saw around them. In Melbourne, for example, the Ladies' Benevolent Society which delivered outdoor relief across the city from 1851 grew out of a Presbyterian Dorcas Society and drew its initial membership from the city's Protestant elite. Similarly, the work of the Melbourne Orphan Asylum began in 1845 when the members of the Anglican St James Visiting Society opened a small home for the deserted children they had encountered in their work. It was only as the enterprises grew that they turned to their husbands and other male supporters to sit on the management committees that dealt with legal, financial, and property matters.

The sectarian battles that scarred the development of public education in Australia flowed over into its charitable institutions. Disputes developed over which clergy should have access to their residents and which forms of prayer would be allowed.[10] The distribution of funds raised in annual Hospital or Charity Sunday appeals was often subject to similarly sectarian tussles.[11] The disputation was at its most extreme in relation to institutions that accommodated women and children. The Protestants argued that Catholics contributed the majority of the residents but few of the donations, while the Catholics complained that they were denied access to minister to the spiritual needs of their co-religionists and that, as a result, their children were

---

[10] See, for example, "Sectarianism and Charity," *The Goulburn Herald and Chronicle*, 12 February 1879, 4, http://nla.gov.au/nla.news-article100876124.

[11] "Charity Sunday," *The Ballarat Star*, 4 October 1881, 2, http://nla.gov.au/nla.news-article202594060; "Hospital Sunday," *The Cumberland Argus and Fruitgrowers Advocate*, 23 August 1890, 6, http://nla.gov.au/nla.news-article86266744.

being brought up as Protestants.[12] The Catholic community's response was to develop its own institutions, often initiated by groups of laymen but eventually staffed and managed by members of religious orders, most of which were brought from overseas specifically for this purpose. Catholics constituted at least one-third of the population in most colonies and were able to use their electoral power to access the assistance governments had already made available to other charities. The earliest such institutions were orphanages, but over time aged care, disability services, and hospitals in which residents were cared for within a Catholic environment were added to the mix. The availability of the religious orders reduced the need for charitable action among lay Catholics. There might have been more scope in the distribution of outdoor relief, but the ladies' benevolent societies with funding to perform this task rarely included Catholic women on their committees. In part, this reflected the sectarian divisions in the communities from which the members were recruited, but practices such as commencing the meetings with prayer also served to exclude Catholic women.[13] Catholic laypeople responded by introducing the St Vincent de Paul Society to provide a similar service to the Catholic poor. The initial branch, founded in Melbourne in 1854, struggled to gather members and lapsed after four years. Later branches emerged in Perth in 1865, Sydney in 1880, Melbourne in 1885, and Tasmania in 1898 completing the segregation of welfare services across

---

[12] "Popish Charity," *The Protestant Standard*, 15 December 1877, 3, http://nla.gov.au/nla.news-article207787048; "Protestant Charity," *Freeman's Journal*, 22 June 1889, 12, http://nla.gov.au/nla.news-article115379884.

[13] "Correspondence," *Record*, 15 August 1896, 3, http://nla.gov.au/nla.news-article108481444; "New Benevolent Society for Richmond," *The Age*, 17 August 1897, 5, http://nla.gov.au/nla.news-article190653261.

Australia. Although membership was restricted to laymen, the introduction of ladies auxiliaries provided an outlet for Catholic women with the time to become involved in charity work.[14]

The success of such Catholic enterprises in safeguarding the most vulnerable of their flock brought a response from Protestants keen to direct their charitable efforts to more open evangelism. The supposedly nondenominational model established by the London City Mission, founded in 1835, was replicated in many colonial cities. Employees of such missions were instructed to relieve the poor of all denominations but to use their visits as a way of introducing them to the principles of Protestant Christianity. "Strictly prohibited from interfering, or even from advising, in matters connected with Church polity," they were nevertheless "required to teach that the blood of the Lord Jesus Christ cleanseth from all Sin; that God loves, and would save all men, and that He will give the gift of His Holy Spirit to all who shall ask it at His hands."[15]

The arrival of the Salvation Army in Australia challenged this interdenominational model. Beginning in Adelaide in 1881 and quickly spreading to Melbourne, Sydney, and Hobart, the Army offered a more sophisticated version of the city mission model, offering an attractive blend of charitable and worship services which funnelled the saved into the new denomination. Its willingness to take advantage of existing government support for voluntary charitable effort saw the Army claim that it was operating thirty-three institutions

---

[14] For the history of the St Vincent de Paul Society in Australia, see S. Frank Egan, *The Society of St. Vincent de Paul in Australia 1854–1954: The First 100 Years* (Sydney: New South Wales State Council, 1981).

[15] "City Mission," *The Courier*, 25 May 1855, 2, http://nla.gov.au/nla.news-article2484291.

by 1898, including industrial, maternity, rescue, and prison gate homes, as well as shelters, slum posts, labour yards, and industrial colonies.[16] The success of the Salvation Army attracted the attention of other Protestant denominations keen to explore its model of evangelizing the poor.[17] Faced with declining congregations in working-class areas, many adopted a model which saw traditional styles of worship abandoned in favour of more popular forms, augmented by a range of welfare services designed to meet other than spiritual needs. In this model the poor were no longer understood as being "in our midst" and were transformed into objects of mission.

The Wesleyan Methodist denomination was the most enthusiastic adopter of the mission model. Drawing their inspiration from the British Forward Movement, churches located in the inner city were reconstituted as Central Missions offering a mix of charitable and evangelical services coordinated by individual charismatic clergymen freed from the circuit system in order to be able to build up their local following. Beginning with William Taylor in Sydney in 1884 and Alexander Edgar in Melbourne in 1893, missions used open-air services, street parades, bands, and orchestras to rebuild their congregations. The aim was to link worship and service, with the churches open seven days a week and ministers actively participating in debates around social policy. The availability of government funding allowed Australian missions to focus particularly on what they called the "social wing," developing a chain of

---

[16] "Foundation of Salvation Army Social Services," https://www.salvationarmy.org.au/en/Who-We-Are/History-and-heritage/Foundation-of-Salvation-Army-social-services/.

[17] See, for example, "Enlargement of the Diaconate," *The Church of England Messenger and Ecclesiastical Gazette for the Diocese of Melbourne and Ballarat*, 23 December 1882, 1, http://nla.gov.au/nla.news-article197131674.

"For I was hungry..."

institutions, ranging from babies' homes to aged care, to meet the needs of the poor.[18]

The adoption of the mission model by other Protestant denominations was more piecemeal. Several denominations opened missions to the Chinese in city centres and for Aboriginal groups in more remote areas. The Anglican Church experimented with mission churches in several cities, although not all went on to develop the range of social services associated with the Wesleyan model. Perhaps the most successful was Melbourne's Mission to Streets and Lanes, founded in 1883. At its peak, it operated a mission house in the "back slums," a school for the poor, institutions for girls and women, and private hospitals under the control of the Australian-born religious order, the Community of the Holy Name.[19] Concerns about the High Church tendencies of this mission saw Evangelicals within the church establish the Mission of St James and St John, which went on to develop its own chain of institutions from 1919.[20]

The most plentiful of these institutions were those catering to children and young people. Protestants looked with some envy at the ability of Catholics to raise poor children in the faith, hinting that they may well have been recruiting

---

[18] There are many histories of individual missions. See, for example, Ivor Bailey, *Mission Story: The Story of the Adelaide Central Mission* (Adelaide: The Mission, 1987); Brian Dickey and Elaine Martin, *Building Community: A History of the Port Adelaide Central Mission* (Adelaide: Port Adelaide Wesley Centre, 1999); Renate Howe and Shurlee Swain, *The Challenge of the City: The Centenary History of Wesley Central Mission 1893–1993* (Melbourne: Hyland House, 1993); Donald Wright, *Mantle of Christ: A History of the Sydney Central Methodist Mission* (St Lucia: University of Queensland Press, 1984).

[19] Lynne Strahan, *Out of the Silence: A Study of a Religious Community for Women* (Melbourne: Oxford University Press, 1988).

[20] Keith Cole, *Commissioned to Care* (Melbourne: Ruskin Press, 1969).

Protestant children as well.[21] In addition to the institutions operated by the Salvation Army and the Central Missions, the Church of England opened orphanages in South Australia from 1860, Western Australia from 1868, New South Wales from 1893, Victoria from 1894, Queensland from 1898, and Tasmania from 1922, and rescue homes in Queensland from 1870, South Australia from 1881, Victoria from 1886, and Tasmania from 1887. The Presbyterian Church ran children's homes in Victoria from 1890, New South Wales from 1911, South Australia from 1924, and Queensland from 1928, and a rescue home in Victoria from 1909.[22] While, initially, few of these homes drew on government support, as government foster care systems came under pressure from the 1920s, state children's departments increasingly came to rely on such institutions to care for their wards, paying for the privilege. Some church-based children's homes also accepted the Indigenous children removed from their families who would later become known as the Stolen Generations and, in the post–World War II years, child migrants sent by fellow religionists in Britain and Malta.[23]

---

[21] "The Church's Charity," *Tasmanian News*, 22 May 1906, 3, http://nla.gov.au/nla.news-article180342567.

[22] For a full listing of these homes, see "Find & Connect: History & Information about Australian Orphanages, Children's Homes & Other Institutions," https://www.findandconnect.gov.au/.

[23] Both of these policies have subsequently been subject to Commonwealth inquiries: Human Rights and Equal Opportunity Commission, *Bringing Them Home: Report of the National Inquiry into the Separation of Aboriginal and Torres Strait Islander Children from Their Families* (Sydney: HREOC, 1997); Australian Senate Community Affairs References Committee, *Forgotten Australians: A Report on Australians Who Experienced Institutional or Out-of-Home Care as Children* (Canberra: Senate Printing Unit, 2004).

The partnership between government and the churches, pioneered in children's services, extended into other areas of welfare provision in the twentieth century. As Stuart Piggin has argued, the Constitution of the Commonwealth of Australia guaranteed a "freedom of religion, not freedom from it."[24] Under the Constitution, the federal government had the power to develop a national social security scheme. But poverty relief and service delivery remained predominantly a state responsibility, with the partnership between government and the churches continuing to be seen as the best way to provide such services. Relief efforts during the 1930s Depression relied heavily on church agencies, with the Central Missions, Salvation Army, and the St Vincent de Paul Societies becoming major centres for the distribution of relief. Local unemployment relief committees looked to the existing church-based social welfare agencies for the expertise they needed to quickly implement their schemes.[25] When the Victorian government, for example, decided to open a camp for unemployed single men at Broadmeadows, it looked to the Salvation Army to undertake the day-to-day management, "with certain assistance from the police in order to ensure discipline."[26] The state government also funded the Army's soup kitchens and extensions to its existing night shelters.[27]

The Depression was also the stage on which several charismatic clergymen were able to build their reputations in

---

[24] Piggin, "Power and Religion in a Modern State," 332.
[25] See, for example, "Unemployment Relief," News, 10 April 1929, 13, http://nla.gov.au/nla.news-article12911556.
[26] "Unemployment Relief," The Age, 14 August 1930, 8, http://nla.gov.au/nla.news-article202457431.
[27] "New Shelter for Workless," The Herald, 12 July 1930, 4, http://nla.gov.au/nla.news-article242808911.

the welfare arena. At St Mark's Anglican Church in Fitzroy, the Rev R.G. Nichols developed a range of services, borrowing the British and American model of the social settlement to recruit middle-class supporters to live and work among the poor. With the onset of the Depression, the settlement became a centre for relief, with Nichols soliciting support through a regular radio program and a magazine he published under the name of Brother Bill. By 1935, he had enough funding to establish a farm at Lysterfield where he trained unemployed boys to work on the land.[28] While Brother Bill's career ended in disgrace, two of his contemporaries were more successful, laying the basis for welfare organisations that continue today.[29] From his inner suburban parish in Sydney, the Rev Robert Hammond reached out to unemployed men, beginning with the establishment of hostels but culminating in the development of Hammondville, a housing scheme for the unemployed in southwest Sydney. As unemployment declined the organisation he had founded moved into aged care and continues to offer services in that area today.[30] In 1933, another Anglican, Fr Gerard Tucker, brought his recently founded Brotherhood of St Laurence from Newcastle to Melbourne, where he supplied a range of services to address the plight of the unemployed. Like Hammond, he saw part of the solution as settling families in a village in outer suburban Carrum, which, as unemployment eased, was similarly transformed into aged care. The Brotherhood also thrived in its Fitzroy base, implementing a program of social action which arose from a

---

[28] "Young Farmers' Section," *Weekly Times*, 27 June 1936, 23, http://nla.gov.au/nla.news-article224855467.

[29] "Obscene Letters Result in Fines," *The Herald*, 19 March 1943, 5, http://nla.gov.au/nla.news-article245964507.

[30] Meredith Lake, *Faith in Action: HammondCare* (Sydney: UNSW Press, 2013).

philosophy of standing alongside the poor and denouncing injustice rather than simply mitigating its impact.[31] This philosophy sometimes led to the Brotherhood taking an oppositional stance, testing the collaborative attitude that had until that point characterised church-state relationships in the welfare field.[32]

In the more affluent postwar era, the relationship between the church and the state initially prospered. A steady flow of state wards more than compensated for the decreasing number of voluntary placements in church children's homes, supplementing the support in cash and kind that continued to flow from local churches. Despite initial concern that the expansion of social security would diminish the need for church welfare services, new opportunities opened up as the federal government looked for partners in ventures in areas such as aged care and marriage guidance. The Aged Persons' Homes Act passed by the Menzies government in 1954 provided a generous subsidy to religious and other voluntary organisations to build small cottages and flats, a subsidy that was increased six years later.[33] The subsidy offered to marriage guidance organisations, most of which were either directly sponsored by churches or had substantial religious representation on their managing committees, was introduced to address some of the churches' concerns about

---

[31] Colin Holden, Richard Trembath, and Judith Brett, *Divine Discontent: The Brotherhood of St Laurence; A History* (North Melbourne: Australian Scholarly Publishing, 2008).

[32] "Defy Law to Show Flaws Remain in Housing Laws," *The Herald*, 7 November 1944, 3, http://nla.gov.au/nla.news-article246008040.

[33] Pat Jalland, *Old Age in Australia: A History* (Melbourne: Melbourne University Press, 2015), 137–38.

the introduction of the Matrimonial Causes Act in 1959.[34] There was little debate before such arrangements were put in place, as church agencies had already pioneered such services and were seen as holding the necessary expertise.

These partnerships continued largely undisturbed until the 1960s. By that time, however, the church-state alliance had begun to fracture as falling rates of church attendance broke the assumed link between religion and good citizenship.[35] The agencies to which the major churches had delegated their welfare responsibilities were becoming more distant and more complex. Central to this shift was the professionalisation of welfare services that began during World War II and intensified in the years that followed. Congregational donations could not meet the increasing costs that a professional workforce demanded, and staff employed on the basis of their expertise were less comfortable with signs of overt religiosity than their predecessors who had been "called" to the work. These changes forced many faith-based agencies and their sponsoring churches to reconsider the nature of their relationship. To what extent was an agency Christian when the bulk of its staff were no longer church members, the bulk of its funding came from government, and few of its clients had any association with organised religion?

During the 1970s, it became clear that the increased dependence on government funding was not a guarantee of survival for church-based agencies. For the first time in the

---

[34] Elaine Martin, *Changing Relationships: Marriage Guidance Council to Relationships Australia* (Adelaide: Relationships Australia [SA], 1998), 5–8.

[35] Howe and Swain, *The Challenge of the City*, 153–54. For a detailed examination of the challenges faced by churches in the 1960s, see David Hilliard, "The Religious Crisis of the 1950s: The Experience of the Australian Churches," *Journal of Religious History* 21, no. 2 (1997): 209–27.

long history of the church-state partnership power lay with government. As long as the government and the churches shared a similar philosophy, this posed no difficulty. But when rifts began to appear, the agencies found themselves in a vulnerable position. The move towards deinstitutionalisation deprived them of the large institutions which had been an important focus for giving. While there was little opposition to the move to redirect services to the places where they were most needed, the new diversified and often preventive programs provided fewer opportunities for the type of volunteer engagement that had sustained links with the parishes in the past. The decision by government to put services out to competitive tender forced denominations to consolidate their offerings, overcoming longstanding rivalries in order to present a more united face. It was harder to build such unity across denominational boundaries, however, so the threat of undercutting was ever-present. Competitive tendering also opened the field to more non-church-based, and increasingly business-based, organisations who shared none of the values that had been central to Christian involvement in welfare.

These threats intensified as the government increasingly embraced values that some within the church-based agencies saw as antithetical to their principles. For many organisations, this challenge has seen a reassertion of the Christian values that had made them uncomfortable in the past, re-embracing their "prophetic voice" in speaking out on behalf of the poor and stepping back from contracts which they argue act against their interests. Influenced by liberation theology, both Catholic and Protestant agencies now, on occasion, take an activist or even oppositional stance, arguing that social justice activism reflects God's preferential option for the poor.[36] The damage done to the reputation of many of these organisations through the revelations of, and consequence inquiries into, institutional abuse also forced a re-evaluation of their past and a reconsideration of the meaning of being a Christian agency.[37]

At the same time, the dismantling of significant elements of the safety net introduced by the federal government in the aftermath of World War II threatened the effectiveness of the outsourcing of charity from the churches to their welfare agencies. Churchgoers accustomed to deflecting their obligations to the poor by donating to denominational charities found that the poor were again in their midst, returning to the churches for relief, bringing their often disrupted lives into the heart of the congregations. Many such congregations have responded by initiating meals programs and youth, refugee, and homeless services, often created without government funding or professional input. These services, however, are being developed in a very different environment from the community initiatives out of which the large church-based agencies still responsible for most of Australia's welfare services originated. While governments are happy to have the churches carry such responsibility they no longer see them as preferential partners but rather as competitors in a market place for government support.

---

[36] See, for example, "Our Faith," Centracare, https://centacarebrisbane.net.au/about/our-faith/; *Others*, no. 14 (2010), https://www.sarmy.org.au/Global/SArmy/Resources/social/others/issues/2010/others-issue-14-oct-2010.pdf; "History & Values," Uniting, https://www.unitingwesley.org.au/history-values/; "About the Brotherhood," Brotherhood of St. Laurence, https://www.bsl.org.au/about/.

[37] The most damaging of these has been the Royal Commission into Institutional Responses to Child Sexual Abuse. See "Final Report," https://www.childabuseroyalcommission.gov.au/final-report.

Diaconal Action on the Basis of Christian Spirituality

Johannes Eurich

If I might define the word "diaconia," it means the helping attention, care, and support of fellow human beings in the spirit of brotherly and sisterly love. It is the spiritually motivated provision of professional help, assistance, and support of people in distress or with specific needs. This helping behaviour has always been a characteristic of the Jewish-Christian tradition, evident already in the Hebrew Bible. In the first centuries of the early Christian church, *Christus medicus* contributed to the attractiveness of the Christian faith. His commitment, grounded in his Christian faith, to care for and support widows and the sick helped distinguish the faith from the wider religio-cultural milieu. This concern for the sick and the poor persisted over the centuries and in nineteenth-century Europe and especially in Germany was a central motivating factor in the development of the modern diaconia movement.

Much has changed since then. Today, this long tradition of Christian diaconia faces specific challenges. Professional standards have developed in addition to, or even as replacements for, Christian motives, and these frequently direct diaconal action without any consideration of the spiritual aspects. The underlying philosophy for these standards often emphasizes individual self-determination and the capacity of all to live independent lives. This framing assumption then informs the general principles of the diaconal organisations or institutions (e.g., in their guiding principles) and finds public expression through the Christian organisational culture or in the mission statement. While the Christian faith continues to play a crucial role in the self-conception of these diaconal institutions and the people involved in this work, such motivations often cause tension with general social developments regarding religious orientation. The decreasing ability of church milieus to attract and retain people and the related increasing number of people working in diaconal organisations who do not have any Christian affiliation means that diaconal staff are themselves characterized by the religious pluralism common within Western societies. Today, not only Christians but also agnostics or Muslims work in diaconal institutions. These developments deeply affect the diaconal self-understanding: what characterises a Christian hospital as Christian? What is the purpose of diaconal institutions in the first place when the services they supply are also offered by secular providers? What is the relationship between this secular approach and the diaconal commitment on the part of church communities?

I approach this problem set by investigating the motives of diaconal action, especially as these are based in and grow out of Christian spirituality. My interest is with the foundations of helping action from a Christian perspective, with reference not only to diaconal institutions but also to the diaconal commitment of church communities. This chapter concludes with an examination of studies on social capital which affirm the importance of religious motives for the ongoing social commitment to fellow human beings.

The Justification of the Human and Christian Love of the Neighbour

The doctrine of justification is a central aspect of the Protestant faith, and it provides strong impulses for the orientation of diaconal action in the spirit of the gospel: God unconditionally accepts and justifies all human beings despite their trespasses. God's love is unlimited and bestowed on all people. Martin Luther's conclusions drawn from this insight are well known: Christians are not, above all, pious people but are to be described in relation to faith and love. In his work *On the Freedom of a Christian* he says: "We conclude therefore that a Christian does not live in oneself, but in Christ, and in his neighbour; in Christ by faith, in his or her neighbour by love. By faith the Christian is carried upwards above himself to God, and by love he sinks back below himself to the neighbour, still always abiding in God and His love."[1] According to the Protestant reformers, faith in Jesus Christ and the practice of this faith through love of neighbour cannot be separated from each other. They attribute great significance to the practice of faith through love—entirely in the spirit of St Paul's dictum that the one who loves the other has fulfilled God's Law (Rom 13:8).

The logical tendency towards a universal ethos[2] of helping others directs diaconal action, obliging us to help people in need irrespective of religious, ethnic, or other differences.

---

[1] Martin Luther, *Luther's Works*, vol. 31: *Career of the Reformer*, ed. Harold J. Grimm (Philadelphia, PA: Fortress Press, 1957), 371.

[2] See Gerd Theißen, "Die Bibel diakonisch lessen: Die Legitimitätskrise des Helfens und der barmherzige Samariter," in *Diakonie – biblische Grundlagen und Orientierungen: Ein Arbeitsbuch*, ed. Gerhard K. Schäfer and Theodor Strohm, 3rd ed. (Heidelberg: Universitätsverlag Winter, 1998), 376–401.

Michael Wolter, a New Testament scholar, describes this internal connection as follows: "In the Christian understanding of reality, which interprets Christ's death on the cross as an integral part of the revelation of God's universal saving will, each human being becomes, as it were, one for whom Christ died. Thus, in this understanding of reality, an identity is attributed to the human being that finds its concretely perceivable expression in the deeds done for this human being—in fact by those who attribute this identity to him."[3] Consequently, a Christological anthropology grounded in the crucifixion perceives one's fellow human being as a human being in whom we encounter Christ himself. Such an anthropology recognises Christ's nakedness in the naked beggar and his hunger in the hunger of the fellow human being; thus, it understands Christian helping action as something that happens between human beings on an equal footing, who encounter each other as brothers and sisters in Jesus Christ. This can have an impact on contemporary forms of helping action and serve as a guiding principle. For example, all forms of super- and subordination that can easily emerge in helping situations, which are in principle asymmetric because a human being needs the help of another human being, are countered on the basis of this equality in Christ. Today, this fundamental principle can have another implication: If all human beings are understood and perceived as brothers and sisters in Jesus Christ, then no one can be excluded from fellowship with God. This promotes a paradigm of inclusion because, in this context, all human beings are accepted in their existence and welcomed

---

[3] Michael Wolter, "Ethisches Subjekt und ethisches Gegenüber: Aspekte aus neutestamentlicher Perspektive," in *Diakonie in der Stadt: Reflexionen – Modelle – Konkretionen*, ed. Heinz Schmidt and Renate Zitt (Stuttgart: Kohlhammer, 2003), 44–50, here 50.

as they are without any obligation to change or to first fulfil special requirements. This has to be practiced today especially with regard to people with disabilities, in order to make a common life in church and society possible.[4]

Based on the acceptance by God and the trust in God's good intentions for God's children, human beings become free—free from all constraints of self-justification and free to perceive and engage with other human beings. The attitude of unrestricted attention and care for the other grows out of that ground; this attitude is important for helping other human beings because it helps prevent the instrumentalisation of helping action and its possible corruption through being used for purposes contrary to the well-being of the other.

The (Diaconal) Shaping of the World as a Consequence of the Protestant Faith

While some theologians ground the Protestant faith in the doctrine of justification, this is but one doctrine beside others which shape the Protestant faith traditions. Of interest here is the Reformation attitude of world affirmation and world responsibility.

The Protestant reformers rediscovered family, work, and society as themselves necessary to a worshipful life[5] and regarded this orientation as fundamental to the shaping of a Christian life. "The 'real' Christian life does not primarily take

---

[4] Johannes Eurich, "Spiritualität und Inklusion," in *Geistesgegenwärtig begleiten: Existenzielle Kommunikation, Spiritualität und Selbstsorge in der Psychiatrie und Behindertenhilfe*, ed. Jörg Armbruster, Nicole Friedmann, and Astrid Giebel (Neukirchen-Vluyn: Neukirchener Verlag, 2014), 7–31, here 21.

[5] Peter Zimmerling, *Evangelische Spiritualität: Wurzeln und Zugänge* (Göttingen: Vandenhoeck & Ruprecht, 2003), 284.

place in the liturgical-meditative sphere, even if this sphere is a constitutive element of that life, or, according to monastic principles, even if these may be helpful, but takes place in the everyday life and at the believer's place in the world."[6]

The Protestant faith is lived through the professional helping action of social workers, caregivers, therapists, assistants, and others who work in the diaconal context. There is no conflict or opposition between spirituality, on the one hand, and the lived mundane reality, on the other. The same applies to diaconia: "Here, piety does not consist in the pursuit of the hidden Christian or even in church-related aims, but in 'objectivity.'"[7] God is present in the professional everyday helping action and acts through the Spirit: "Whenever in the biblical tradition God's loving attention manifests itself through human beings, the texts speak of the Spirit of God. It is this profane and entirely technical, and so the personal empathic care and attention by doctors, caregivers, Christians, Muslims, other religious people, and close or more distant people, through which the accompanying and comforting presence of God reveals itself."[8] From the Christian perspective, any helping action can be a medium through which God's love is revealed. God has wholly and unconditionally committed God's self to human beings and is present not only in the individual areas of their lives but also in all highs and

---

[6] Hans-Martin Barth, *Spiritualität* (Göttingen: Vandenhoeck & Ruprecht, 1993), 51.

[7] Barth, *Spiritualität*, 51; see Dietrich von Oppen, *Der sachliche Mensch: Frömmigkeit am Ende des 20. Jahrhunderts* (Stuttgart: Kreuz-Verlag, 1968).

[8] Günter Thomas, "Behinderung als Teil der guten Schöpfung? Fragen und Beobachtungen im Horizont der Inklusionsdebatte," in *Behinderung – Profile inklusiver Theologie, Diakonie und Kirche*, ed. Johannes Eurich and Andreas Lob-Hüdepohl (Stuttgart: Kohlhammer, 2014), 67–97, here 87.

lows of human life. The Christian faith is not a spiritualised belief but a visible manifestation of faith in the lived life.[9] In his letters from prison, Dietrich Bonhoeffer provided an example of such a spiritual attitude. With regard to his life, Bonhoeffer stated that he did not want "to become a saint" but to "learn to have faith."[10] The Christian faith's relatedness to this-worldliness finds expression in the orientation towards the suffering of the creation and towards the dedication of one's own life to the shaping of this world in the presence of God. To continue with Bonhoeffer:

> I discovered later, and I'm still discovering right up to this moment, that it is only by living completely in this world that one learns to have faith. One must completely abandon any attempt to make something of oneself, whether it be a saint, or a converted sinner, or a churchman [or woman] (a so-called priestly type!), a righteous person or an unrighteous one, a sick or a healthy one. By this-worldliness I mean living unreservedly in life's duties, problems, successes and failures, experiences and perplexities. In doing so, we throw ourselves completely into the arms of God, taking seriously, not our own sufferings, but those of God in the world—watching with Christ in Gethsemane.[11]

This fundamental orientation towards God's will for this world and the coming of God's kingdom directs attention towards the development of this world, which manifests itself in an attitude of watchfulness in the context of social

---

[9] Wolfgang Huber, "'In deinem Lichte schauen wir das Licht': Quellen und Perspektiven christlicher Spiritualität," Festvortrag zum 25jährigen Jubiläum des Stifts Urach, http://www.ekd.de/vortraege/huber/051022_huber_urach.html.
[10] Dietrich Bonhoeffer, *Letters and Papers from Prison*, ed. Eberhard Bethge, 2nd ed. (London: SCM, 1971), 369.
[11] Bonhoeffer, *Letters and Papers*, 369.

responsibility. This attitude is reflected both in a commitment to and a living "in an abundance of tasks, questions, successes and failures"[12] and in opposition to a one-sided orientation towards other social values such as success, physical beauty, or power, because these erode the principle of humanity and marginalise vulnerable people.[13] Christian spirituality strengthens the inner sensibility which time and again helps to recognise what is beneficial, and what is detrimental, to life. It raises its voice against the commercialisation of life and the "commercialisation of the soul."[14] Christian spirituality cares for the bruised reed, practices solidarity with the weak, and recognises God in compassion and mercy. To quote a well-known expression by the French bishop Jacques Gaillot: "Those who immerse themselves in God, emerge beside the poor."[15] Christian faith cannot be separated from solidarity with the disadvantaged and marginalised in the world. It sets an example and serves as a counterweight to the culture of utilisation, self-indulgence, and materialism of our times. "In our societies, the pressure to control and exploit everything has almost become a religious obligation. Therefore, religion must be a counterforce to halt this pressure."[16]

---

[12] Bonhoeffer, *Letters and Papers*, 369.
[13] Gottfried Claß, "Aspekte diakonischer Spiritualität," in *Diakonische Konturen: Theologie im Kontext sozialer Arbeit*, ed. Volker Herrmann, Rainer Merz, and Heinz Schmidt (Heidelberg: Universitätsverlag Winter, 2003), 277–91, here 289.
[14] Huber, "In deinem Lichte schauen wir das Licht," 1.
[15] Cited in Fulbert Steffensky, "Suche nach spiritueller Erfahrung," *Neue Wege: Beiträge zu Religion und Sozialismus* 99, no. 7/8 (2005): 221–28, here 225.
[16] Claß, "Aspekte diakonischer Spiritualität," 288.

Christian Spirituality and Diaconal Action

Christian faith or Christian spirituality includes this adoption of an inner attitude towards the world and so to orient one's action in the world towards diaconal service. In the following I would like to explore this relation in more depth.

Faith means counting each human being as one for whom Christ died. By seeing Christ's eyes in the eyes of the poor and the sick, one learns to recognise the "other face of things." In this way a different relation to the creation and the things that surround us comes into being: Spirituality teaches us to feel deep emotion and reverence for life and is aware of the harm done to creation. "Spirituality is an attitude which focuses on life and strengthens and protects it against all mechanisms of death," says Leonardo Boff.[17] It represents an attitude that venerates all things in life as a gift and not taking them for granted, using them carelessly, or subjugating them to its own purposes. The question as to how the world can be shaped through faith is inextricably connected with questions such as: How can I perceive and become aware of things? "How can I recognise and understand the pain of human beings and how am I touched by this pain? How do I deal with the things of everyday life? Am I capable of venerating them as gifts or do I only use and instrumentalise the world?"[18] This attitude of awareness and attentiveness becomes even more important as technical procedures and methods play an increasingly important role in medical treatment and patient care. Despite

---

[17] Cited in Cornelia Coenen-Marx, "Dem Geist Gottes Raum geben: Spiritualität als diakonische praxis pietatis," in *Spiritualität in der Diakonie: Anstöße zur Erneuerung christlicher Kernkompetenz*, ed. Beate Hofmann and Michael Schibilsky (Stuttgart: Kohlhammer, 2001), 47–61, here 54.

[18] Coenen-Marx, "Dem Geist Gottes Raum geben," 54.

all the technical devices employed in this context, in direct contact with patients, medical therapy and care are nurtured by "the ability to recognise changes in the patient's smell, body temperature, voice, or overall impression."[19] A spiritual approach of awareness and attentiveness can help one really to perceive fellow human beings, to pay careful attention to their vital signs, and to search for possibilities to support and strengthen their acceptance of life.

Especially in the context of diaconia, Christian spirituality respects the dimension of the human lived body because it embraces the human person in his or her totality and therefore in his or her embodied life. Christian spirituality tries to perceive the human person and to answer his or her needs against the background of his or her lived life. Consequently, in this context, giving care does not represent a mere act of caring for bodily needs or of tranquilising the mind. To provide care for a human being means establishing a relationship and recognizing the person in his or her suchness, to concede the person the right to need help, and to give the person in his or her helplessness what is needed and what will help and do good. "Where a human being of flesh and blood becomes transparent for God, diaconal work becomes a challenge which also changes the one who gives help."[20]

This can happen in two ways. On the one hand, being moved and touched by the other can result in contemplating one's own life, in becoming more aware of the things in life, and possibly in rediscovering how to lead one's life. This enables a fresh access to faith and a new understanding of biblical texts—experience-oriented and undogmatic. This

---

[19] Coenen-Marx, "Dem Geist Gottes Raum geben," 54.
[20] Coenen-Marx, "Dem Geist Gottes Raum geben," 55.

diaconal *praxis pietatis* changes the perspective on our everyday life: a good meal with friends, a journey to a foreign country, a beautiful garment, convalescence after an illness—all this is a gift. To accept it is part of having mercy for oneself.[21]

On the other hand, being moved and touched by the other can result in sealing oneself off. "Any true contact with a human being of flesh and blood makes us vulnerable."[22] A natural reaction to this is to protect oneself and build up walls around one's vulnerability because—especially as a professional caregiver—it is not possible to bear every suffering and distress. Inner exhaustion and burnout would be the inevitable consequence. Sealing oneself off and creating an inner indifference or insensibility bear the risk, however, of missing the possibility of a successful encounter with the other and of ignoring the signs of God's presence in everyday life. Especially within the framework of diaconal action, which, due to the value of efficiency, is subject to organisational pressure, it is more difficult to pause and reflect.

Under the predetermined conditions—for instance, time pressure in patient care—it is a challenge not to succumb to an instrumentalisation of life. "We know that," says Cornelia Coenen-Marx, "[b]ut who has the time to listen to the questions behind the questions? The caregivers? Rarely. The respiratory therapist or the physical therapist? Maybe. The hospital chaplain? There are many dialogue partners—but who really establishes a relationship?"[23] Under time constraints and against the pressures of utilization, the freedom to pause and reflect is something to be fought for or deliberately

---

[21] Coenen-Marx, "Dem Geist Gottes Raum geben," 58. Emphasis in the original.
[22] Sam Keen cited in Coenen-Marx, "Dem Geist Gottes Raum geben," 58.
[23] Coenen-Marx, "Dem Geist Gottes Raum geben," 53.

created. This challenge should not, however, be imposed on the individual, on caregivers, for example, without creating appropriate possibilities (concerning time) for developing such moments. Rather, this challenge is one of management responsibility and has to be handled on the structural level by shaping the organisational culture in a spiritual way.[24] We do not need to start from nothing in this regard. A number of different approaches have already been successfully tested in practice. Through a culture of pausing and reflection, of existential communication, of prayer, etc., these seek to create a "Christian-spiritual corporate culture"[25] that gives employees a free possibility of developing a profound spiritual contemplation and approach to diaconal action.[26]

Diaconal Action in Civil Society

To this point, the focus has been on the connection between Christian faith and the diaconal commitment in the world and this either from the perspective of the individual believer or with reference to diaconal institutions. What remains to be analysed is the diaconal dimension of church community work. Such church communities are gathered under the heading "civil society" because nowadays the church is described as an organisation that is integrated into and operating under the conditions of civil society.

---

[24] See Beate Hofmann, *Diakonische Unternehmenskultur: Handbuch für Führungskräfte*, 2nd ed (Stuttgart: Kohlhammer, 2010).
[25] See Joachim Reber, *Christlich-spirituelle Unternehmenskultur* (Stuttgart: Kohlhammer, 2013).
[26] See also vol. 1 and vol. 2 of the series *Geistesgegenwärtig pflegen* (Neukirchen-Vluyn: Neukirchener Verlag, 2012–2013).

One often hears a number of programmatic formulas which capture this assumption: For example, "[t]he church is either a diaconal church or it is not a church at all."[27] This affirms that the main social commitment of congregations is to the local community2[28] and within, for instance, the framework of community organising.[29] The cooperation between church communities involved in community-related activities and diaconal institutions assume a central importance.

Community-related diaconia represents the following:

> a form of the church's diaconal work, which is jointly carried out by church communities and districts as well as diaconal service providers and institutions and which also involves other actors. Community-related diaconia focuses on the neighbourhood, orients itself towards the situation of the people who live there and thus opens up towards the community. Joint action of the institutionalised church and organised diaconia requires a strategic cooperation, in order to find a balance between

---

[27] Karl-Fritz Daiber, "Volkskirche der Zukunft – eine diakonische Kirche?," in *Religion in Kirche und Gesellschaft: theologische und soziologische Studien zur Präsenz von Religion in der gegenwärtigen Kultur* (Stuttgart: Kohlhammer, 1997), 275.

[28] See Volker Herrmann and Martin Horstmann, eds., *Wichern drei – gemeinwesendiakonische Impulse* (Neukirchen-Vluyn: Neukirchener Verlag, 2010); Kirchenamt der Evangelischen Kirche in Deutschland, ed., *Herz und Mund und Tat und Leben, Grundlagen, Aufgaben und Zukunftsperspektiven der Diakonie: Eine evangelische Denkschrift* (Gütersloh: Gütersloher Verlagshaus, 1998), 67; and *Kirche der Freiheit. Perspektiven für die Evangelische Kirche im 21. Jahrhundert. Ein Impulspapier des Rates der EKD* (Hannover 2006), 81; Diakonisches Werk der EKD, ed., *Die Rolle der Allgemeinen Sozialarbeit im Rahmen gemeinde- und gemeinwesenorientierten Handelns in der Diakonie (G2–Modell)* (Stuttgart, 2007).

[29] Hanns-Stephan Haas, *Enabling Community, Gemeinwesen zur Inklusion befähigen: Elf Empfehlungen für innovatives Handeln in Kommunalpolitik, Verwaltung und Soziale Arbeit* (Hamburg: Evangelische Stiftung Alsterdorf, 2009).

the orientation towards customers, members, and the community.[30]

Therefore, this approach makes particular demands on the church and diaconia.

On the one hand, the becoming-diaconal being of church communities "still represents the essential question as to their identity."[31] The mission of the churches is to communicate the gospel within concrete everyday world contexts, that is, within the very different areas of life in late modern societies. Answers to existential questions are especially sought in conflict-laden and distressful life situations.

> As a consequence, the favoured places of Christian preaching are no longer the pulpit and the lectern but the public hedges and fences that structure and shape the landscape of discourse and action in modern societies; hedges and fences in interactive landscapes, where people publicly talk about everything and anything, and where the life force which is connected to the testimony of faith in the Christian God is proven in practice and comes true through the "silent testimony" of the helping deed.[32]

The "silent testimony of the helping deed" is not to be separated from faith in the God of Jesus Christ. By virtue of their declared faith in God, it is necessary for churches to be

---

[30] Martin Horstmann and Elke Neuhausen, *Mutig mittendri: Gemeinwesendiakonie in Deutschland; Eine Studie des sozialwissenschaftlichen Instituts der EKD* (Münster: LIT Verlag, 2010), 5.

[31] Andreas Lob-Hüdepohl, "Zivilgesellschaft als 'Tatlandschaften' – Sozialethische Anmerkungen zur Gestaltungsmacht zivilgesellschaftlicher Akteure," in *Zukunft verantworten – Teilhabe gestalten: Zivilgesellschaftliche Impulse Gustav Werners*, ed. Lothar Bauer, Johannes Eurich, and Heinz Schmidt (Heidelberg: Universitätsverlag Winter, 2012), 60.

[32] Lob-Hüdepohl, "Zivilgesellschaft," 61.

part of civil society.[33] "There they provide civil society–related diaconal services in two respects: as diaconia *for* or *as a service* to civil society, if they integrate the semantic potential of Christian preaching as well as the powerful silent testimonies into the civil public's discourses of self-understanding and into its shaping actions—through educational-cultural, political-ethical, and social-charitable diaconia."[34] The contribution of churches for the benefit of civil publics becomes concrete, for instance, in communicating a "culture of help."[35] This phrase refers to the forms of acceptance and awareness and attentiveness, of the internal connection between mercy and justice, of solidarity with the poor and the marginalised, of possibilities of failure and guilt, and of forgiveness and reconciliation. This potential represents a specifically religious contribution and results from the Christian notion of the human as a being created in the image and likeness of God who is capable of answering and is therefore responsible.

On the other hand, the churches depend on diaconia *within* the civil society so as to constitute themselves as communities of faith in a concretely experienceable social form. This, of course, does not represent the churches' only or even primary social form. It is, however, a social form which makes the church experienceable and tangible for people who otherwise have no direct contact to a church anymore. Here, civil

---

[33] See Andreas Lob-Hüdepohl, "Kirche in der Welt? Theologische Bemerkungen zum Verhältnis von Gottesbekenntnis und öffentlichem Wirken der Kirche heute," in *Kirche zwischen Staat und Zivilgesellschaft*, ed. Rupert Graf Strachwitz, Frank Adloff, Susanna Schmidt, and Marie-Luise Schneider (Berlin: Maecenata, 2002), 42–61.
[34] Lob-Hüdepohl, "Zivilgesellschaft," 61.
[35] See Wolfgang Huber, *Kirche in der Zeitenwende. Gesellschaftlicher Wandel und Erneuerung der Kirche* (Gütersloh 1999).

society–related processes provide possibilities to bring to bear genuine church traditions and life patterns. "This is because individual undertaking of life-related skills—also those of church members who already are part of the church through christening—evolve today more than ever within the sphere of public communication and action."[36] The church's specific civil society–related diaconal modes not only represent a contribution to the civil public's self-understanding and opinion-forming processes but also enable the church to establish its diaconal projects within the structural frameworks of the civil society's sphere of action. By this means it is possible for the church to communicate its message to its own members, and to others who want to hear it, and to constitute itself in that way.[37]

Examples of community organising, in which parishes and charitable organisations have also taken part, demonstrate the practical promise this approach affords.[38] In this context, there are good opportunities for cooperation and interaction between an organised entrepreneurial diaconia and the church community's voluntary commitment. Church communities could find here an access point to their fundamental diaconal dimension or even strengthen existing modes of diaconal expression. A church community might not only commit itself (more strongly) to its local social environment ("outward de-limitation") but also become aware of its own inner variety and neediness, which may to this point have remained concealed ("inward de-limitation").[39]

---

[36] Lob-Hüdepohl, "Zivilgesellschaft," 61.
[37] Lob-Hüdepohl, "Zivilgesellschaft," 61f.
[38] See Eugen Baldas, ed., *Community Organizing: Menschen gestalten ihren Sozialraum* (Freiburg: Lambertus, 2010).
[39] Lob-Hüdepohl, "Zivilgesellschaft," 62.

The Significance of Christian Faith for the Social Capital of Society

As a final observation, religious faith is demonstrated to be of great significance for social commitment to one another.[40] Within the German context studies have shown that churches are helpful in forming attitudes which are beneficial for civil society: "religious institutions, which see their task in advocating for the weak and in supporting a culture of benevolence, seem to be 'training spheres' of prosocial orientation."[41] If this is the case, one should not be surprised by the considerable impact churches have on the number of volunteers in society. According to the statistics produced by the German Federal Ministry for Family Affairs, Senior Citizens, Women and Youth, there are over 4 million volunteers in the context of the two major churches in Germany.[42] Similar

---

[40] In this section, I rely on Gregor Etzelmüller, "Religious Communities, Churches and Civil Society," in *Church and Civil Society: German and South African Perspectives*, ed. Michael Walker, Nico Koopman, and Koos Vorster (Bloemfontein: Sun Press, 2017), 107–26.

[41] Sigrid Roßteutscher, *Religion, Zivilgesellschaft, Demokratie: Eine international vergleichende Studie zur Natur religiöser Märkte und der demokratischen Rolle religiöser Zivilgesellschaften* (Baden-Baden: Nomos, 2009), 423. Translation by the author.

[42] See Bundesministerium für Familie, Senioren, Frauen und Jugend, *Bericht zur Lage und zu den Perspektiven des bürgerschaftlichen Engagements in Deutschland* (Berlin: Wissenschaftszentrum Berlin für Sozialforschung, 2009), 84.

findings have appeared in the German voluntary survey[43] and the commitment atlas.[44]

One might add to this other striking results from sociological research undertaken in Protestant countries such as the United States and Scandinavian countries and in traditionally Catholic societies such as Ireland, Poland, or Portugal.[45] Protestants who are committed to church community life show more engagement in civil society than active Catholics.[46] This is supported by studies on the concept of social capital. One such study concludes that the reason for the stronger Protestant activity in civil society is the organisational structure of Protestant communities, which are usually smaller and organised in a more democratic way: "Protestant and Catholic churches differ....Protestant congregations tend, on average, to be smaller; most Protestant denominations allow for greater lay participation in the liturgy; and most Protestant denominations are organized on a congregational rather than hierarchical basis."[47] Roßteutscher concludes that organisational

---

[43] Bundesministerium für Familie, Senioren, Frauen und Jugend, *Freiwilliges Engagement in Deutschland 1999–2004: Ergebnisse der repräsentativen Trenderhebung zu Ehrenamt, Freiwilligenarbeit und bürgerschaftlichem Engagement* (München: VS Verlag für Sozialwissenschaften, 2005).

[44] See "Engagementatlas 2009: Daten, Hintergründe, wirtschaftlicher Nutzen," http://zukunftsfonds.generali-deutschland.de/online/portal/gdinternet/zukunftsfonds/content/314342/309588.

[45] See Richard Traunmüller, *Religiöse Vielfalt, Sozialkapital und gesellschaftlicher Zusammenhalt: Religionsmonitor – verstehen was verbindet* (Gütersloh: Verlag BertelsmannStiftung, 2014); Richard Traunmüller, *Religion und Sozialkapital: Ein doppelter Kulturvergleich* (Wiesbaden: VS Verlag für Sozialwissenschaften, 2012).

[46] Etzelmüller, *Religiöse Vielfalt*, 7.

[47] Sidney Verba, Kay Lehman Schlozman, and Henry E. Brady, *Voice and Equality: Civic Voluntarism in American Politics* (Cambridge, MA: Harvard University Press, 2002), 245.

patterns lie at the core of the differences between Catholics and Protestants: The evident difference is not the result of direct "ideological-theological origins."[48] One might question this conclusion given the influence that doctrine has over organisational structures, hierarchies, etc., but her general findings remain of interest. Overall, one may say that in our Western societies Christian churches remain one of the major actors fostering positive attitudes towards the common good and providing an unusually large number of socially engaged volunteers. If churches can connect this great potential with diaconal organisations, both can have a lasting impact on society.

---

[48] Roßteutscher, *Religion, Zivilgesellschaft, Demokratie*, 68.

Agencies and Congregations: Who Is the "Other" in Our Relationship and Why?

Lucy Morris

"The greatest temptation to which world religions frequently succumb is to devolve either into mere instruments of procuring bread or into weapons in worldly struggles which are largely about bread as well."[1]

Context

In considering the "Other," the challenge is always to be alert to the myriad opportunities to reverse that gaze and look away from the Other. Agencies in Australia today face a range of challenges in their relationships with civil society, governments, businesses, each other, and those who need their services, many of whom constitute the Other. This need to focus on the Other comes to the surface over any and every issue when there is a lack of awareness and commitment to think through implications for the organisation's character. This might include, for example, a discussion about an agency's asylum seeker and refugee advocacy policy, even

---

[1] Miroslav Volf, *Flourishing: Why We Need Religion in a Globalised World* (New Haven, CT: Yale University Press, 2015), 23.

though that agency does not deliver those particular services at the present time.

The price of advocacy over contested issues is high when public or governmental tolerance is low. Countercultural activity is fraught with risk. The way the agency needs to "be" in the role of advocate as a faith-based and nonviolent activist organisation is hard to discern, and it can be complicated to come up with a shared, accepted, and integrated approach going forward. Each person around the table has her or his own perspective, preferences, and level of willingness to take a risk. It is more than simply developing a fresh policy for the organisation; instead, it is about relationships and the willingness, or its lack, to compromise on what was a core characteristic in his or her values, vision, and mission. The imperative remains, however, to so consider the Other for, as Arundhati Roy, has observed:

> The trouble is that once you see it, you can't unsee it. And once you've seen it, keeping quiet, saying nothing, becomes as political an act as speaking out. There's no innocence. Either way, you're accountable.[2]

This reality of what we see and how we respond is at the heart of my discussion.

This chapter on the role of the Other in the relationship between congregation and agency in the community benefit sector comes predominantly from a CEO perspective, with the author having direct and significant leadership experience in Anglican, Roman Catholic, Baptist, and secular not-for-profits

---

[2] Arundhati Roy, *The Algebra of Infinite Justice* (London: HarperCollins, 2002), 172. Roy was referring to the issue of use and misuse of power in circumstances of peace and war.

or community benefit organisations and within the Anglican Church as a priest.

In board discussions, what emerges are the passions, current and past practices and roles, the ever-present risk and capacity to lead and manage in straitened times, a review of the strategy, the organisational vision, and the religious faith which all come together in a debate that is never quite resolved. Some leaders today try to co-create a new future and fresh responses to the world's needs with their stakeholders, while others simply settle for surviving using custom and practice to determine the way ahead.

Yet to consider the Other remains unsettling; the Other is irritatingly visible and will not go away. The compromises made must be told and shared, to enable understanding and awareness about what has to be tackled and changed. We need to expand the boundaries on our current limits. It is this mixture of visioning and hope, resistance and engagement, pragmatic service obligations to customers and stakeholders to meet contractual and quality service obligations, faith expectations and current economics which offers us this ongoing, unresolvable, productive tension.

Nor is there a definitive answer about who is among the Other at any point in time. This remains a constantly evolving narrative that stretches and tests the network of relationships as they acknowledge and tackle the issues.

Globalisation

These critical relationships are framed within the context of today's globalised, connected world, with our current cultural, social, and economic contexts, including the essential one of "good governance." Community agencies automatically recognise and accept the constraints and opportunities arising from this broad, sweeping, all-encompassing context, along with the myriad definitions and situational agreements on the identification of the Others determined by our governments and politics, business imperatives, civil society, and church congregations.

In one reading of the postmodern context, human beings are individual, autonomous, and personally responsible for their own "selves," personal futures, successes, and failures. It is the globalised world's default position in how society and individuals understand their faith, privileging their God and God's creation.

This context has herded and driven agencies into becoming outsourced agents of governments. It defines what services are delivered, the organisational structures and systems, the character and expectations of the current tranche of leadership, the sector's business and working relationships, and the identity of the Other.

It is a world that appears vastly different from anything ever seen before. Our language, our business analytics, our communications, our brands, and our methods and types of employment have all changed and are continuing to change at a rapid pace. Jobs previously reliably embedded in community sector agencies and in society more broadly are disappearing without trace. New skills and new economic realities are emerging.[3]

Priorities are also changing. Work is changing. Labour and employment are changing. Contracts are reducing. Human dignity has a price which even faith-based systems can find hard to resist. What is emerging from the shadows are micro

---

[3] Naomi Klein, *Shock Doctrine* (Australia: Penguin Group, 2007).

contracts, bonded labour deals, below minimum wages, and highly profitable service contracts and business models for companies who get in at the ground floor for the first three to six years. By then, the profitability has been squeezed and there is none left. The contracts are dumped and those who can move on, while the for-purpose agencies struggle on.

This confluence of forces has stimulated a pragmatic acceptance of human trafficking and slavery as a direct consequence of the drive for bigger profits and agreements and a default acceptance about the uses to which surplus humanity might be put, with abusive contracts such as managing off-shore detention centres or environmentally destructive extractive industries.[4]

Fear, Faith, and Money

Ours is a world divided into "haves" and "have-nots" as our capitalistic practices entrench difference and divides. Once again, fear is a predominant driver for decision making politically, socially, and economically.

This is also applied in our faith decisions. Money appears to be the most accepted criteria for defining success, along with youth, race, and gender—the big privileged categories. The Other, by contrast, comes to be what is feared the most and the easiest to label and confine as well as to maintain control and exercise power over.

Narrow performative capacity and professional technocratic management now constitutes the sum total of the new leadership aspirations and character in agencies. This reduces

---

[4] Kevin Bales, *Disposable People: New Slavery in the Global Economy*, 3rd ed. (Oakland: University of California Press, 2012).

our expectations of leaders to those who can claim to be capable and competent in exclusively measurable ways.[5] Today, agencies are appointing technocratic management leaders, who frequently lack in soul and substance, merely reflecting back into society the narrative society already knows and accepts as unchangeable norm.

This has become a key challenge for boards as they choose their CEOs and watch their levels of risk aversion rise, while the costs and risks emerge differently from the past and without a proven recipe for the future. As governments seek to evade any risk by passing it on through outsourcing services, it is deliberately initiating the death throes of small and single-purpose agencies which have limited resources and so limited capacity to change. These agencies find themselves unable to respond.

Communications

To cope with these rapid changes and the growing demands being made on them, it is not uncommon for agencies to retreat into telling simplistic stories to engage with the social, cultural, and economic constructs. Both congregations and agencies are distracted with the need for survival and measuring the current indicators of success, while occasionally and spectacularly losing their way with decisions made about survival and growth at any cost: like, for example, chasing after contracts and service options and going against its own original mandate, vision, mission, and values.

---

[5] Donna Baines et al., "Self-Monitoring, Self-Blaming, Self-Sacrificing Workers: Gendered Managerialism in the Non-Profit Sector," *Women's Studies International Forum* 35, no. 5 (2012), 362–71.

The need to be sustainable is an essential concern for boards given the corporate penalties and governance standards steadily being implemented for professional board directors and CEOs and in the expectations from their customers. It must be recognised that the current structure of charities and faith-based systems is not ensured and that changes are already upon them, irrespective of any preparation or understanding. This results in a critical need for different constitutions, ways of maintaining independence and generating funds, and the design and implementation of new organisational structures

Understanding and accepting these changes will open up new opportunities. Now is the ideal opportunity for change. It is time for agencies and congregations to redefine and refresh their relationships for their next chapter.

A New World...

For Arundhati Roy, "[a]nother world is not only possible, she's on the way and, on a quiet day, if you listen very carefully you can hear her breathe."[6] It is possible to hear her breathing when this challenge is approached from a faith perspective. This sound will unite the sector and its people together with the churches and congregations. It will strengthen them as it has done traditionally. And, if it does not, it will reduce us to the divisions of "Empire"—to use Arundhati Roy's terminology—colluding in and colonised by Empire.

---

[6] Arundhati Roy, *The Chequebook and the Cruise-Missile* (London: Harper Perennial, 2004), xii–xiii. From a speech titled "Confronting Empire," delivered at the World Social Forum in Porto Allegre, 28 January 2003, and it became famous for the vision it inspired.

In other words, it is this point of agreement which will enable the sector and its leaders to change from being the third arm of government where it has been residing for the last thirty or forty years. During this period, the sector has swallowed, like the python eating an elephant, the promise of steady funding and traded in its independence and advocacy, giving ourselves almost terminal indigestion along with the ephemeral belief of funding reliability. All the while, the sector has steadily removed God from the marketplace and relegated God to the ranks of the Other, the alien, the stranger, the scapegoat.

These changes now enable us to speak directly to those purchasing services and allow us to choose to work with those who are unable to access the system, with those who are only able to work for the "gleanings of the field" (Ruth 2:1-18).[7] Instead of the government always claiming the role of customer, NGOs and faith-based agencies can work with service users as the rightful and welcomed customers.

It will allow everyone in the sector to keep their priorities clear and not be absorbed or colonised by those with other agendas. The sector will be able to take a longer-term, generational view of the world, going beyond governments into a more personal and inclusive civil society. It allows a very different quality of decision to be made than one determined simply by business and economic criteria.

---

[7] The story of Ruth includes the Jewish practice of the owners leaving the edges of the fields free from harvesting for the widows and orphans to harvest. It allowed the poor and impoverished to collect what was left over from the harvest to prevent starvation and pointed towards a more generous and less greedy way of living in the community and in God's creation. There is enough for all.

Any refusal of the sector to see or accept this challenge is what, in the end, will undo the community services sector, agencies, and congregations and reduce them to invisibility and irrelevance. As agencies they will come to an end in their current structure and systems if they respond in like manner to the framing expectations governing today's powers and authorities. Following this path may provide a short-term quick fix, but, in the long term, it leads to dilution and diminishment in service provision.

It is interesting to debate this in a purely secular environment, where faith is privatised and the language of faith and religion is no longer recognised, understood, or accepted. But the sector itself is well served by faith-based agencies and these agencies are able to companion both their brothers and sisters in the congregations and their customers. There is a visible and urgent need for a far closer relationship between agencies and congregations than the increasingly distant one suggested by the current rhetoric. The challenge presented by this position for people who are not faithful or who have had no experience of faith should be our starting point in the relationship, not the point of rejection. In this complex space, seeing into a relational future of a shared, faithful community comprising both agency and congregation is essential for survival and flourishing. It is where the most hope emerges. For the congregations and agencies to be active in enabling humanity to flourish in God's kingdom, once again everyone must be prepared to take risks and see and do things differently if there is going to be a harvest.

Our Shared Relationship

CEOs and leaders in the community benefit sector have often observed that the additional web of relationships embedded in the heart of faith-based organisations, with their auspicing or sponsoring congregations, can be among the most precious—but they can also be the most fractious, resented, tense, and misunderstood. They can be supportive, alive, relevant, courageous, hope-filled, companioning, and engaged even to death—and dysfunctional, incapable, abusive, discriminatory, completely misaligned, and blind.

Any reflection on the relationship between agencies and congregations, when it is at its most fraught and tense, demonstrates the fundamental nature of the concerns being addressed: power and control over the services, the nature of the gospel message, the people who are employed, the assets, the services, the reputation, and the contribution to the kingdom of God and their implications for the religious institutions, the faith, and the faithful.

For some, the image adorning the ceiling of the Sistine Chapel with Adam barely touching fingers with God defines and frames a better relationship, sort of "there" and visible but not too close, within touching distance but not involved or interdependent, in fact, barely companioning. But agency and church leaders must be prepared and point to a different way of being, doing, and measuring success that is also qualitative, outcomes-based, relational, just, compassionate, and humble and in this way demonstrates the incredible extent of the gospel's countercultural narrative. This, at least, encourages a shift in the use and understanding of power and reduces the surplus powerlessness that is driving all of us into disengagement, anger, frustration, fear, and violence. This difference, this opportunity to be different in our services within this postmodern narrative of autonomy, will assist the future of both agencies and congregations.

Boards and Leaders—Good Governance

In the relationships with boards of faith-based entities, there is often a constitutional obligation and relationship already on paper. Some forms of this relationship will be closer than others. Some are still owned by the church itself, which has remained as the employer. This results in quasi-independent "boards" which still report to and are accountable to the congregation or diocese.

Those who are truly responsible as the religious head of the structure, whether bishop, archbishop, assembly, or synod, have authority, in theory, to approve the appointments made to the agency's board. The challenge for the chairperson and the relevant congregational leader is to bring in people with business capacity and good intellect but also people who have the vision, mission, and values of the organisation in their hearts as well as their minds, who are active in the faith, and who will never bow to the demands of Empire at the cost of God. Holding that balance both in congregational and in agency leadership is the challenge in a secular environment.

Today, CEOs have moved significantly beyond novel or new practice, or the simplistic acceptance of "best practice," or even the notion of complicated practice. Instead, they have become practitioners in what is called complex and emergent practice: essentially the identification of challenges that are always relational, between the key stakeholders, without a right or wrong answer, aiming always to move the conversation and issues along, working with what works while it works. In the relationships between congregations and agencies, there is never a point at which either group can claim to have arrived.

The Acts of the Apostles tells stories of dissension, debate, and agreed difference. This reminds us why it is so hard to build community in life-sustaining ways when we become fearful and colonised as part of the Empire and the secular world. Difference can reduce our focus to matters that divide rather than what unites. Being unwilling to walk in the shoes of the Other, as congregation or agency, leads to separation rather than companionship.

The willingness to live and work outside the circles of power on a regular basis is essential in both groups as it means the stories of the marginalised are never silenced and help inform practice and passion for change, for justice, and for hope.

Agencies are frequently challenged when their prophetic witnessing is at odds with the hard realities of government contracts, when theological positions are at odds with community expectations of services, and when the political influence determines theology rather than the other way around. Enabling difference to flourish with inclusive diversity and genuine love for the Other is the way to transform organisations and congregations. Managing the financial risk is essential in both spaces.

CEOs and leaders find it hard to believe that God's will is being done on Earth. We continue to behave and act as though this time is God-free and hang on to what already exists before being in a place to respond to God. The personal survival instinct responds to evident threat, and this leads people to live their lives without faith and hope in spite of what might be said or done.

Temptation

Miroslav Volf has observed that "[t]he greatest temptation to which world religions frequently succumb is to devolve either into mere instruments of procuring bread or into weapons in worldly struggles which are largely about bread as well."[8] Congregations have been enormously influential in the founding stories of faith-based agencies, providing the means for delivering essential services which were not provided by governments or which were at odds with government policies of the day (refugees and asylum seekers, HIV/AIDS sufferers, family and domestic violence victims and perpetrators). As a consequence of this service, people's lives were changed for the better. God was and is present in the work. In the midst of all the change and challenge, prophetic witness has taken place among the staff, volunteers, customers, families, communities, and governments.

But the agency system has also developed in ways that are sometimes almost antithetical to its original mandate. Particularly in Australia and in spite of the best of intentions, charities have frequently become very white, male, middle-class, privileged responses to poverty and need.

Keeping a Balance—As the World Changes around Us

The notion of operating in the margins, among the gleanings of the field, has ceased to be a valid option within the structures and systems of organisations or churches as those institutions struggle for funding, recognition, and survival. Persuading governments to allow policy space and capacity for NGOs to

---

[8] Volf, *Flourishing*, 23. The temptation always for agencies is to chase after the money in order to survive, but this often comes at the cost of vision integrity. Agencies can become direct service deliverers without analysing and witnessing to the fundamental principles behind the causes of the poverty and struggle.

operate with a faith and social justice licence in the gleanings of the fields is becoming harder and harder.

In the last thirty to forty years, profound changes have occurred in the community benefit sector in Australia. From its inception, it has been a sector with a significant, visible church presence in the wide range of social services. A good deal of funding came from congregations, and it was embedded in communities, with large volunteer support systems and employees working for minimal wages. Over time, the funding model shifted so that agencies are now funded predominantly by government. They have become a de facto third arm of government and are now constrained by the regulations, values, and direction demanded by the government.

Agencies are a very cheap alternative to the more expensive option: governmental direct delivery of human services. No open market was able to compete with the low wages and cheaper choices. By the mid-1990s, government funding was meant to cover 75 percent of the costs with the rest volunteered, fundraised, and donated by the church and its supporters. It was a good deal for governments and congregations. Services were provided to those who were unvalued economically, the poor, the unemployed, the homeless, the disabled, the sick and dying, the elderly, children, and those imprisoned. Here was precisely where the congregations' mandate drove the faith-based organisations. It was a partnership in which church and state both benefitted.

In more recent times, as government funding has increased and expectations from society have changed, human services have become far more professional. Extensive training, management expertise, financial acumen, and risk management have shifted in-house in response to successive governments' complete outsourcing of all risk. This has occurred alongside the almost silent and unacknowledged fight for gender equality within this system. The prevailing structure and policy supported a welfare system that kept women marginalised, forced to accept lower work status, deprived of opportunity, and unable to criticise the quality of the services being provided.[9]

This shift to professionalisation is reinforced by the increasing interest of those working in government and the corporate sector: as wages rise and status and reputation increase, the rewards and promises being made to professional employees are very different from those promoted thirty or forty years ago. More people are now looking to the NGO sector for career opportunities. It is a similar story with boards and board membership because the sector is looking more economically profitable and so has greater political, social, and cultural capital.

Developments in this direction continue apace, as agencies turn themselves into human service retail operators, preparing to compete within a rapidly emerging marketplace where commerce and trade now occur within, around, and through human services.[10] The capacity to become competitive in this space is now the number one priority, drowning out any other message or memory of lessons learned from previous changes. Flexibility, innovation, entrepreneurship, and "user pays" represent the drumbeat of the new message. This means almost all human services are subject to the impact of commerce, trade, and profit demands. There is money to be

---

[9] Lucy Morris, *Valuable Charities, Invaluable Women: A Feminist Critique of the Role of Women in Charitable Organisations* (Saarbrücken: VDM Verlag Dr. Muller, 2007).

[10] Colin Cremin, *Capitalism's New Clothes: Enterprise, Ethics and Enjoyment in Times of Crisis* (London: Plutobooks, 2011).

made out of poverty and misery. This occurs both directly and indirectly, as evidenced by the growing presence of stateless, virtual, and sovereign multinational corporations which are able to achieve economies of scale previously only dreamed of, beyond the reach of accountability to local stakeholders and governments.[11] Governments are preferring these options as they remove and outsource risk and accountability and help keep prices down.

As markets are created and opened to the winds of competition, it feeds the self-fulfilling belief in individual autonomy, self-reliance, and entitlement. The key loss here is in understanding that this is all God's creation: the rewards of personal efforts and the opportunities from which each person benefits all come from God and go back to God, continuing to flow on to all God's people.

In this self-contained world, as an individual, the overriding message is that we succeed or fail through our own efforts and merit. Each person's carefully managed brand and capacity to self-advertise is critical in establishing a small space in which they might be seen, in which they might gain employment, create a career, gain wealth to live, achieve a recognisable reputation, and maintain a wealthy successful life. This definition of life and living has been translated into agencies' survival stories, character, values, and visions.

For faith-based agencies, the temptation and practise are to privatize and marketize God. God's brand is not always seen as helpful or easy to understand. For those who work in faith-based agencies or who worship in the congregations, being open about believing in a living and

---

[11] Anthony Elliot and Charles Lemert, *The New Individualism: The Emotional Costs of Globalization* (Oxon, UK: Routledge, 2006).

acting God is a real risk and no longer acceptable in many contemporary workplaces. Insistent marketing mantra brand managers advise CEOs to remove all reference to God from agency names: "People are put off by it, no longer identify with it; it has become old fashioned and irrelevant; it's not inclusive and not welcoming." This rebranding does afford agencies some distance in the case of blow-back from the churches' poor handling of human relationships, people's lives and choices and judgement, and the appalling abuse scandals. It is easier to change the look of the agency to make it more modern and accessible and make God an optional choice. With that, the preferential option for poor also becomes optional.

Counterculture...

We need to find and tell other stories, stories of faith-based agencies living and working in the edges of the fields, helping to glean, helping to stand in solidarity, and witnessing to the state of the nation and the world. These are countercultural stories which enable people to step into the future with optimism, providing strong brand recognition, relevance, and funding in response to the courage and reconciliation that is offered. As counterintuitive as it may now appear, those agencies which remain hand in hand with congregations have a better chance of survival.

The "faith/identity spectrum" is one way of evaluating the form and extent of the relationship. At one end of the spectrum stands a completely secular agency. At the other, the agency is identified as explicitly religious.[12] Most faith-based agencies land somewhere in the middle. There is often a faith background which is honoured as part of the tradition and founding story but which has retained little influence on the current and future practices. There may be a more practiced and identified faith affiliation, but staff are not expected to be Christian and are more likely to be humanistic. Generosity and acts of kindness provide the lens through which the values are practiced. It is a stretch for such agencies to consider themselves faith-centred.

The more distant form of relationship a congregation might have with its sister agency occurs when the congregation suspects that the agency risks the dilution of the faith profile and the congregation's "brand." The agency is understood to be a little less reliable and trustworthy and questionable as a useful companion and partner. This response works both ways. The next step becomes one of managing risk, either through seeking a wider separation or greater control—an unsatisfactory approach as neither approach deals with the presenting issues of a shared vision and story.

One way forward is to understand that there is a wide range of permissible faith profiles in both contexts. It is possible to see that agencies mirror what is found in congregations. Not only is faith not always present, but the distinctive character of the faith and its overall belief structure are varied. An agency should be the mission arm of the congregation, which is auspicing and sponsoring the agency and supporting,

---

[12] See Ronald J. Sider and Heidi R. Unruh, "Typology of Religious Characteristics of Social Service and Educational Organizations and Programs," *Nonprofit and Voluntary Sector Quarterly* 33, no. 1 (2004): 109–34.

companioning, sharing, and co-creating alongside and with them. Neither group should ever move away from the other.

Boards, leadership, management, and the faith-based agency should always be active participants in and influenced by the faith journey. It is important to have about 30 percent of those in leadership and key influencing roles active in the faith; approximately one-third of the community should be faithful to affect the culture, vision, mission, and values. Clarity and agreement about roles and responsibilities when agencies and congregations work together is essential and needs to be renegotiated regularly.

The new world for both congregation and agency is one of networked, interdependent, and intra-dependent relationships. Issues of power, influence, language, and communications are what will make or break the future well-being of both. The vision and storytelling of the gospel, discipleship, and the work of those who walk in these footsteps will provide the cradle for these conversations and understanding.

If there is no larger vision, there is no reason to remain close. If there is no reason to remain close, contentious issues of policy undermine the relationship. Without a basic shared vision, over time small disagreements and differences accumulate and do not dissipate. These instead become rocks on which a shipwreck occurs. It is likely to be as simple as that!

Re-Membering the Body:
Six Theses on Congregation, Church Agencies, and the Ecclesia of God

Stephen Pickard

The capacity to grasp the breadth and depth of its own life with God in the world is one of the key challenges before the contemporary church. This is inherently difficult to achieve. One strategy for coping with this complex being of the church in the world is to identify, differentiate, and develop particular dimensions of the church's life and witness. The emergence of welfare agencies belongs to this natural splitting process. The strategy becomes highly problematic, however, when the various sectors of the Body of Christ lose their connection with each other. Agencies can easily become seduced by external pressures and opportunities and forfeit their inner ecclesial identity. Congregations, shorn of their links to their orientation to the world, risk forfeiting their missional relevance. The subtle and powerful dialectic between identity and relevance becomes subverted in a fractured church. This chapter maps some of the dynamics associated with the above developments. In doing so, it examines the relationship between the different modes in which ecclesial life and witness has to be undertaken. This is explored through six theses.

The quest for a more integrative ecclesiology in which identity and relevance operate in reciprocal relation will necessarily involve a faithful and costly re-membering of the Body of Christ. This is a minimal requirement in order for the church and its various welfare and educational agencies to offer an authentic embodiment of the gospel of God in the world.

Thesis One: *A major challenge for the contemporary church is to grasp the breadth and depth of its own life with God in the world. This is inherently difficult to achieve.*

Beyond the ills, failures, and puzzles of the contemporary church in the West there is a more significant challenge that is never named or, for that matter, believed. Put simply, the fundamental challenge for the church of God is how to cope with the abundance of divine life in the world. This, of course, might seem a nonsense given the daily reports of violence, institutional fragmentation, and human suffering in the world. Yet the Christian Gospels—which are read in most of the world's mainline churches regularly, if not weekly—offer a counterintuitive reading of the world. In the encounters of Jesus there is an abundance of life, healing, and new possibilities. Indeed, it is so intense at times that it cannot be contained, generating significant strong reactions both for and against that abundance. Coping with the abundance of God's blessing is indeed a challenge.

I begin with this proposal because it is entirely germane to the current issues that arise from the familiar splits developing between the churches and the welfare agencies they birthed. I want to approach this particular issue from a distinctly ecclesiological point of view. We are in urgent need of a more intentional and adequate ecclesiological framework within which to clarify and understand much of our present predicament. It might not be immediately apparent why the abundance of God is a theological issue at the heart of much of our present difficulties regarding the relationships between church, agency, government, but I do wish to attend to this in what follows.

Alongside the above proposal there is a further foundational axiom that seems equally implausible to our ears today, both for those of the church and for those who have nothing whatsoever to do with the church. Our desire for human companionship (which I take to be reasonably uncontested and in fact well documented from a variety of disciplines) somehow involves seeking God, and our search for God similarly involves an attraction to others.[1] More often than not today, involving God in our search for companionship appears as an optional extra for those so inclined either by birth, upbringing, persuasion, or modest inclination, perhaps occasioned by some significant life experience. Moreover, I say "our desire for human companionship *somehow* involves seeking God" because the way God belongs to our seeking and finding the company of others is complex and rich and belongs to the deepest wonders of being a creature of God.

The simple yet profound insight into the interconnectedness between the move towards God and to one another comes from the fourth-century monastic Dorotheos of Gaza. He described the pathway to God and others in the following way:

> Suppose we were to take a compass and insert the point and draw the outline of a circle. The centre point is the same distance from any point on the circumference....Let us suppose that this circle is the world and that God is the centre; the straight lines drawn from the circumference to the centre are the lives of [human beings]....To move toward God we move from the circumference along the various radii of the circle to the centre. But at the same

---

[1] See chapter 1 in Stephen Pickard, *Seeking the Church: An Introduction to Ecclesiology* (London: SCM, 2012).

time, the closer they are to God, the closer they become to one another; and the closer they are to one another, the closer they become to God.[2]

For Dorotheos, seeking the company of God and others went hand in hand. Here is a simple clue to what being the church is all about. It involves a desire for God and a corresponding desire for one another. One contemporary theologian of the church speaks about this journey towards God in terms of attraction:

> Creatures are created to move towards God. When creatures somehow lose that towardness—becoming obsessive at some point, separating from the whole of things and serving only themselves—then the creation loses its order. To lack attraction to others and to God is to suffer the inertia of self-attraction: in Luther's terms, to be "twisted into self."[3]

The Spirit of God, who empowers human beings and God to come into closer relation, is the same Spirit at work between human beings drawing them closer to each other. The Spirit works in both directions simultaneously. This means that the experience of human empowerment through deeper shared life is never just a human achievement but also a work of the Spirit, who is between all things drawing all things into the holiness of God. As human beings find their life together in God, they share a foretaste of the coming kingdom. It is earthed in the here and now. It is a foretaste and provisional, but nonetheless genuine.

---

[2] See Roberta Bondi, *To Pray and to Love: Conversations on Prayer with the Early Church* (Minneapolis, MN: Fortress Press, 1991), 14f.

[3] Daniel W. Hardy with Deborah Hardy Ford, Peter Ochs, and David Ford, *Wording a Radiance: Parting Conversations on God and the Church* (London: SCM, 2012), 47.

To reiterate, our movement towards God is correlated to our movement towards one another. These two moves are simultaneous and generative of community with God and each other. Even if this proposal commends itself to you, it will probably jar somewhat when stated in the following form: *to seek God and one another is simultaneously to be a seeker of the church*. In the Christian tradition, the God sought is the Triune God of love. To be a seeker of such a God will necessarily lead into deeper communion with the world of this God and its peoples. From this perspective, the study of the church and the life and practice of faith concerns a journey into the unmeasurable "height, length, depth and breadth of the God of love" (Eph 3:18), a journey undertaken in the company of others.

One way to formulate this divine–human attraction as it relates to the church is as follows: "All God's creatures are moved by God to their fulfilment in him; the Church is doubly so moved, as one among God's creatures and as a creature that embodies that movement for others."[4] This statement captures the divine initiative underlying the movement towards God and each other. It also brings into focus the sense that the church embodies this movement in its own life. Unbelievable perhaps that seeking God, seeking one another, and embodying this search through the life of the church (at least as we might know it and or experience it) are mutually involving and that these three are together at the heart of our spiritual quest. It goes against the grain in a social environment aptly described as one of "pick 'n' mix religions"

---

[4] Robert W. Jenson, *Systematic Theology II: The Works of God* (New York: Oxford University Press, 1999), 172.

uncoupled from traditional institutional forms of belief and practice.[5]

In the Christian tradition, seeking God is a shared activity which involves companionship with others. It is for this reason that the Roman Catholic theologian Karl Rahner stated: "a Christian has to be an ecclesial Christian."[6] And it is clear—at least logically from what I have argued above—that an ecclesial Christianity is one that is necessarily woven into the very fabric of the world where God is present and active. Being the church necessarily means being involved in multiple engagements informed by God's active wisdom in the world. If we want to consider the domain of the church we will necessarily have to work hard at "assembling all that is needed to promote the fullness of human society."[7] Clearly, that is a complex and demanding task. The life of church ought to have an osmotic and dynamic feel about it that is always orientated beyond its own life, always reaching deeper into the world of which it is a creature in its own particular way. In this sense, we are wise to focus not on who is *in* or *out* of the church but on who is *of* the church. And we ought to give careful attention to demonstrating how and why blurred boundaries between the church and society are to be expected and embraced.

It ought to be abundantly clear from my first thesis that the twin challenges of (a) the sheer abundance of God in the world and (b) the deep theological connection between seeking God, seeking one another, and being the church are highly complex realities. Grasping the fullness of such a web

---

[5] Bryan S. Turner, *Religion and Modern Society* (Cambridge: Cambridge University Press, 2011), 205.
[6] Karl Rahner, *Foundations of Christian Faith: An Introduction to the Idea of Christianity* (London: Darton, Longman & Todd, 1978), 345.
[7] Hardy, *Wording a Radiance*, 79.

of relations, human and divine, is beyond any one person or social entity. And here is the deep predicament for the church. It cannot fully grasp its own life; it is always more than what it appears, richer than what it might seem because its life is hidden with Christ in God and, I might add, "in the world." The very complexity and richness of the life of the church as a window through which the multifaceted and rich wisdom of God might be experienced can be overwhelming (Eph 3:10). This leads to my second thesis.

Thesis Two: *One strategy for coping with this complex being of the church in the world is to identify, differentiate, and develop particular dimensions of the church's life and witness.*

The natural complexity of the life of the Body of Christ in the world is not simply a sociological phenomenon. It is, in the first instance, a theological reality. How to cope with this reality is a major challenge. More frequently this inner complexity is ignored, with one consequence being that it is too easy to make oversimplified critiques of the institutional life of the church. What we singularly fail to do is take with utmost seriousness the richness and complexity of being the Body of Christ in the world. Various options present themselves to cope with this complexity. One option is to develop a theological rationale for a highly structured and top-down institution. This top-down causality and control offers tight boundaries, coherent policies, and clear trajectories. But, of course, it often fails to properly connect at the ground level. Another option is to privilege the local and particular. This approach can attend to the immediate but suffers significant ecclesial fragmentation.

Beyond these various options for dealing with ecclesial complexity, it is important to recognize that there are two co-related dimensions of the church's life in the world. These two dimensions relate to the churches' fundamental concerns for worship and mission. A healthy and vibrant church is one that functions well on both fronts. One scholar refers to these two dimensions in terms of the church in intensity mode and the church in extensity mode.

Intensity mode refers to the church's concentration as a worshipping community. The sacramental life of the church and its attention to proclamation through word and sacrament, song and praise, teaching and fellowship provide the engine for the release of spiritual energy. When the church functions in intensity mode it is attending to its particularity, attending to those fundamental elements generative of its identity. This accords with God's concentrated holy presence.[8] The church in intensity mode comes to explicit and maximal form in worship of the Triune God. On this account, liturgy—and in particular the Eucharist—can be understood as a concentrated mediation on the world's encounter with Christ and the Spirit. Precisely because it is a concentration point, it is not the whole but a genuine instance of what society might become as the church expands though its own inner dynamism in the Spirit.

When the focus shifts from intensity to extensity mode, attention moves beyond the church's sacramental worshipping life towards the world. In this mode, sacraments have to be lived in the world; in this mode, proclamation takes multiple forms through witness in word and deed. In this mode, the church is focused on outward-directed action. This signals a move from particularity to reach, from preoccupation with

---

[8] The distinction between the church in "intensity" and "extensity" mode is developed by Daniel Hardy, *Finding the Church: The Dynamic Truth of Anglicanism* (London: SCM, 2007), 109–13.

identity to preoccupation with relevance. Here we note that the reach of the church is essentially unbounded and capable of significant expansion under the impress of its life in the eschatological Spirit. The role of the Spirit patterning the life of Jesus offers a theological clue. Luke's Gospel is a good example, for here, in the life of Jesus of Nazareth, the Spirit overshadows, comes upon, descends on, fills, leads, empowers, is released, and raises Christ. In the same way, in the Acts of the Apostles the Spirit of the Father's Son is the agent that comes upon, fills, leads, empowers, and raises the people of the Messiah. It also means that the church can be that mode of sociality, which brings into focus the holiness of God in Christ. The form of the church follows the form of the impress of the Spirit patterning Christ. This means that the church's life is constantly propelled outward, crossing boundaries, reconstituting persons, place, and society in the process. It means that who is "of the church" is an open matter. On this account the church is an unfinished eschatological mystery, which remains in constant movement beyond preestablished boundaries. This is a critical feature of what a renewed sociality looks like and a criterion for discernment of a static or dynamic ecclesiology.

Here, then, are two fundamental modes of existence for the church of Jesus Christ. Understanding these two modes in terms of intensity and extensity offers a way to understand the dynamics of the complex and rich (both sociologically and theologically) nature of the Body of Christ. In a very general and not absolute way we might identify these two modes thus: intensity mode attends to identity and particularity; extensity attends to relevance and reach. For the church to be the church both modes of existence have to be dynamically related and mutually enhancing. It is only as they are so aligned and dialectically related that worship and mission feed each other and become modes through which the Spirit of God seeks, attracts, gathers, and releases the people of God for work and witness in the world.

Thesis Three: *The emergence of welfare agencies belongs to this dynamic ecclesial process embracing worship and mission.*

I have tried to offer a theological and ecclesiological framework for the dynamics of church life in the world. This is important because without it we remain blind to the reasons for many things and fail to understand why some things happen or take the course they do. Within the above dynamic ecclesiology, it is quite understandable that the churches will have to order their internal and external life in such a way that maximizes their capacity to reach out from the particularity of their internal identity. The emergence of welfare agencies and related entities of the church can be understood within this dynamic ecclesiology. The history of such developments in Australia is rich and interesting. In any case, the purpose here is not to rehearse or track such developments. History shows how and why welfare agencies arose, and it is clear how this related to the missionary purposes of the churches of Australia.

The move into extensity mode is, of course, a contingent matter and displays all the intrigue and passion that accompanies the missional and political realities of churches often divided and at loggerheads with each other in this country. The competitive nature of a divided Protestantism and a powerful Roman Catholicism significantly impacted on the form and fortunes of the development of welfare agencies in Australia. However, that the church developed such outreach and extended its reach into the places of deepest need ought not be surprising but rather happily recognized and admired. But the very dynamic which provided the rationale and energy for such developments also harboured within it dangers which are an inevitable consequence of the church's missionary and service orientation in obedience to the gospel.

Thesis Four: *The strategy becomes highly problematic when the various sectors of the Body of Christ lose their connection with each other. Agencies can easily become seduced by external pressures and opportunities and forfeit their inner ecclesial identity.*

The above developments are seriously compromised or become dysfunctional when the dialectic between the church in intensity and extensity mode is no longer recognized or promoted in practical ways. Of course, this not a particularly new problem. For example, the main issue for the church at Corinth appears to have been a failure to discern the body in its various parts. The gifts of the Spirit for the building up of the body become embedded in particular persons and/or cliques (e.g., the spirituals). This church was in danger of being twisted in on itself and unable to attend to what made for the good of the whole, for the flourishing of the Body of Christ in the world. Preoccupation with self-identity subsumed the gathering and outward-directed movement of the Spirit. Worship and what happened in worship appears to have become quite consuming. Even in these early days of the church the delicate ecology of intensity and extensity in the ecclesia of God was easily disrupted.

A danger arises when the natural movement out into the world, a movement of mission and service responding to human need, becomes disconnected from the internal life of the church. The church in extensity mode is always tending to dispersal, entropy, and associated loss of energy.

This is natural. It is also the reason why it needs to remain firmly embedded in its sacramental life and attentive to Holy Scripture. Without that dynamic connection the threat for the church is that it will dissolve into its host culture. The values and ideals of the host culture (consumerist, competitive) will soon overwhelm the church's reach into the world. Agencies can easily become seduced by external pressures and opportunities and forfeit their inner ecclesial identity. It is difficult to resist this development when there is such a significant loss of connection with the energetics of life in intensity mode. The energy now comes from elsewhere, and the natural human inclination to manufacture its own self-importance and achievements in a competitive environment has all the hallmarks of a distinctly Pelagian temper. The patterning of life according to the discipline of the Holy Spirit is lost to consciousness.

Of course, there is a complementary danger for the church when it becomes shorn of its links to the world. Preoccupation with the intensity of its life simply twists the church even further in on itself. It will be choked not by the cares of the world but by its own inner life. The more identity is bolstered internally, the greater the risk of being severed from the mission. In this context the church ceases to extend its reach. It ceases to be relevant. It ceases to be a church in mission or extensity mode. These are the conditions for the development of a sect-type way of being church. Under such conditions sharp boundaries are drawn between church and world. The inner life of the church is overly sacralised, and it no longer has a practical life in the world to remind it that God's work and wisdom are to be found incarnated in the world. When this occurs, the Pelagian temper gives way to a distinctly Manichaean view of the world in which there is a sharp distinction between the church and the world. Church agencies exist for mission in a world that is dark and lost. This is not how it is viewed, however, by those serving in such an environment. They often see matters very differently. From the church agency's point of view, it is more often the institutional and overly bureaucratic church preoccupied with its own survival that has lost its way. On this account, the agencies are the means of salvation, not simply for the world, but for the church!

Thesis Five: *To repair the broken lines between church and agency requires both to move beyond self-engagement, to suffer interruption and displacement of self-interest, to turn away from self-attraction, to recover a common desire towards the kingdom of God.*

When agencies become so engaged with their own existence that they cease being attracted towards the fullness of life marked by the kingdom, it is a sign that they have settled for some lesser goal—however laudable and admirable that may be. This may not happen immediately but over time. To the extent that the direction of the vision and work of the agency becomes dissociated from its source, or that it becomes enclosed in an endless round of competitive grants for dwindling funds (with all the compliance and legal requirements), it is inevitable that the concern of the agency will be subsumed within or captured by the needs and desires of its host cultures.

In terms of the earlier discussion of extensity and reach, what happens, oddly enough, is that the movement outwards into areas of need can falter or be thwarted by obstacles inherent in the very requirements of the host culture. This can sap energy, and entropy sets in. Two things occur. First, the agency no longer has the capacity or in some cases the desire to extend its reach and movement deeper into areas of need. Second, it does not know how to reconnect to its source. Theologically, what is required is a reestablishment of the agencies' movement towards redemptive life.

The above problems also appear in the churches, though in somewhat different guises. Their preoccupations and self-attractions work against their inner charism. This can happen to such an extent that their own source of energy and life entropies. Disconnection from their originative source and associated loss of movement towards dispersion in the world generate a morbid state that neither feeds nor is fed by anything external. Luther's "twisted into self" assumes an ecclesial form.[9] Such self-preoccupation is not the preserve of the morbid church. It also emerges in highly activist assemblies which draw on resources and sources of energy in a draining manner. Such church dynamics eventually entropy and mutate into entities that are no longer drawn towards God.

Repair of the broken lines requires a form of institutional metanoia, a turning outwards beyond to recognize the fullness of the Body of Christ and its vocation in the world. But what exactly does this look like institutionally? This is not easy to identify. Usually it will involve a shift from preoccupation with structure and reengagement with originative energies. The former is the familiar default position of social life in the West. It is not enough to simply repeat the vision without reorientation and concentration on the deepest sources of the energies of an institution's life.

Thesis Six: *The quest for a more integrative ecclesiology in which identity and relevance operate in reciprocal relation will necessarily involve a faithful and costly re-membering of the Body of Christ.*

---

[9] See Hardy, *Wording a Radiance*, 47.

To summarise the argument to this point: the members of the Body of Christ need to be put back together again. It needs to be re-membered. This has to occur on multiple fronts: practical and theoretical (biblical/theological/ecclesial/sacramental). How might we speak of this from a theological point of view? What might an integrative ecclesiology look like? I have been greatly assisted in this in recent years by the image of the three altars of God in a sermon by the fourth-century preacher and writer St. John Chrysostom (347–407), archbishop of Constantinople (modern-day Istanbul), one of the great cities of the ancient world.

Chrysostom was known for his eloquence in preaching and public speaking. He was a fierce denouncer of wealth, envy and greed, and abuse of authority by both ecclesiastical and political leaders. He had a saying: "As a moth gnaws a garment, so doth envy consume a person." This "prophet of charity" gained a reputation as the "golden mouth" of the ancient world. Chrysostom above all was an advocate for the poor and a constant thorn in the side of the wealthy. His seven sermons on Lazarus and the rich man, addressing the themes of wealth and poverty, are justly famous from the early church.[10]

In one of Chrysostom's sermons on poverty based on the Apostle Paul's first letter to the church at Corinth (1 Cor 9), he is concerned to connect the church's eucharistic worship with the poor of the world. His point was quite simple: What is the point of week-in week-out breaking bread, sharing a common cup to remember the One whose life was given for others, if this has no connection to what is happening in the

---

[10] *St. John Chrysostom on Wealth and Poverty*, trans. Catherine P. Roth (Crestwood, NY: St Vladimir's Seminary Press, 1984).

world to those in need. It is an age-old issue and a very real contemporary issue. Chrysostom addresses it head-on. He promotes a practical Christianity but desires a principled practice.

His theology is a robust defence of Christ's love for the poor. And he needs to make his case because of the apathy, ignorance, and prejudice of the wealthy of the great city of Constantinople. Chrysostom appeals to the image of the altar.[11] The first altar is the altar of Christ's cross and resurrection. The stone that was rolled away from the tomb becomes the new stone of the altar of Christ. This new altar is prefigured in the Old Testament on which the sacrifices were offered. With the coming of Christ the stone altar of Old Testament sacrifice is radicalized. Christ becomes the new altar. Through Christ's sacrifice he forms from the stone altar of ancient times a new living body. The altar of the cross—Christ's life of loving service and sacrifice comes to finality in the cross. It is the basis of our life. We owe everything to the altar of the cross, and it gives our life meaning and purpose. However, the cross of Christ has no independent existence, free floating above and beyond the world lost in some cyberspace of the mind.

Rather, the *altar of the cross* is "refracted, as it were, into two closely connected altars."[12] There is the stone altar made up of the ecclesial Body of Christ. This is an altar of thanksgiving (this is the meaning of the word "Eucharist"); it is the sacrament of salvation and healing. This is the *second altar*. But

---

[11] "The Homilies of St. John Chrysostom: Homily 20," in *Nicene and Post-Nicene Fathers of the Christian Church*, ed. Philip Schaff (Edinburgh: T&T Clark, 1989), 12:372–74.

[12] J. M. R. Tillard, *Flesh of the Church, Flesh of Christ: At the Sources of the Ecclesiology of Communion* (Collegeville, MN: Liturgical Press, 2001), 69.

the altar on which the Eucharist is celebrated is simply stone, and those who gather at this altar remain stony hearted if they are not connected to a *third altar*—the altar of the poor. What makes this second altar of the Body of Christ more "awesome" than the altar of the Old Testament is not simply Christ but the poor who make the altar of the ecclesial body "more awesome." In other words, the altar of the cross expresses itself practically in two altars that are set up in the world.

Chrysostom asks: How can the church remember Jesus who gave his life that the world might live if that same church forgets the world that is in need and the world that Christ came to save? The altar of the sacrament has to express itself in the altar of the poor. There are three altars; they are all related, and each has a place in the kingdom of God; without the third altar of the poor, the cross and the Eucharist are diminished. Or, from a different point of view, the Eucharist that celebrates Christ's life and sacrifice is not complete until the church as Body of Christ offers its sacrifice on the altar of the poor. Here is the final altar that shines a light on the Eucharist and Christ's life.

Chrysostom was critical of the church of his day because, on the one hand, it honoured the stone altar "because it receives Christ's body," but, on the other hand, that same church treats with contempt "those who are themselves the body of Christ...as they die." He is talking about the poor. The poor "are the most sacred part of the altar 'made' by the Eucharist." He says, "[y]ou can see that altar [of the poor] everywhere, lying in the lanes and market places." He observes that while the priest invokes the Spirit at the Eucharist the people of God invoke that same Spirit "not by speech but by deeds because nothing so kindles and sustains the fire of the

Spirit as this oil [of sacrifice at the altar of the poor] poured out in abundance."

Conclusion: Recovering the Three Altars of God

The church of the three altars is the church that responds to the challenge of living in intensity and extensity mode. This is the church that seeks both identity and relevance, the church that drills down into its own particularity and opens its arms in loving reach towards the world. By extension, as the agencies of the church invest in their core mission and seek the altar of the needy in the world, these same agencies illuminate, enhance, and complete the identity and mission of the church that gathers at the Eucharist. The Body of Christ formed from the cross of Christ, the Body that gathers at the altar of Christ, always includes the altar of the needy. It is the poor and needy who make the Eucharist real. Every consecration of the bread and wine at the altar of the Eucharist is simultaneously a consecration of the ecclesial body to a life of sacrifice at the altar of the needy of the world.

The three altars need to be put back together. In truth, it is really only one altar under three forms. The problem we face today is the dislocation and fragmenting of the altars of God's kingdom. The reintegrations required are not easy, but without this the body remains split. The repair required is not simply structural. It will occur only as agencies and churches follow the direction of the energies of their life and being. This following more deeply into the reality of their lives and vocations is a redemptive movement towards the kingdom of God. As such, it is an intensely spiritual movement and is the only kind of movement that will overcome the split and give sufficient power and capacity for the church to recover its founding charism and disentangle itself from the unhealthy aspects of its host cultures.

Henceforth, it matters little whether it is high church or low church, charismatic or contemplative, word focused or social activist—everything depends on whether it is *true* church. And the litmus test of the church's truthful remembering of Jesus will be its sacrifice at the altar of the poor and needy. However, working at the third altar can be exhausting, and people are easily burnt out; they can lose energy, even despair at times or become mesmerized by the allurements of the host culture, its values and treasures. The body count at the third altar can take its toll. Moreover, policies and practices of government and state, and the powers of global corporations that squeeze the life-blood from the least, are often overwhelming. This is why it is so critical and urgent that the ecclesia of God needs to be re-membered as the Body of Christ. An integrative Christian practice includes an appropriate element of transcendence, reminding us that we do not live and work in our strength. There is a resource, a source of renewable energy that is found as people gather to remember the living God in their midst. Even our best work at the third altar can become another form of self-love unless it is given back to the Lord for a blessing and renewal.

Beyond Religious Congregations and Secular Welfare: An Experiment in Uniting Church Ecclesiology

Geoff Thompson

In his Carlyle lectures at Oxford University in 2003, American political theorist Mark Lilla declared that we Western liberal democratic nations are living through a political experiment. He is not referring to any particularly recent experiment. He's referring to the nature of politics in the West over the last three hundred or so years. His argument is that the characteristic feature of post-Enlightenment Western political theory and practice has been to think about and execute politics on our own without any recourse to the idea of God's will or sovereignty. Moreover, this experiment has involved actively resisting attempts to give God or revelation any place in political theory or practice. For these several centuries, Western political theory has, by definition, been determined by publicly accessible objective reason. In matters political, the "secular" (this new conceptual invention of the modern West)[1] would trump "religion" (the other new conceptual invention

---

[1] See, for instance, the much-quoted opening line of John Milbank's *Theology and Social Theory: Beyond Secular Reason* (Oxford: Blackwell, 1990), 1: "Once, there was no secular." Of course, the word "secular" existed previously as a theological concept referring to the time between creation and eschaton. In its modern version, it came to refer to a cultural domain or space in which God, faith, and revelation were excluded.

of the modern West).² Except with the secular's occasional nod to something called the Almighty, or through the banal use of prayers at the opening of parliaments, religion was excluded from the public domain.

None of this is particularly original. Lilla's analysis is interesting, however, in the way he draws attention to just how historically unusual we modern Western liberals are: "Time and again we must remind ourselves that we are living in an experiment, that we are the exception."³ Trying to do politics without religion is such a novel thing that we have not really appreciated what we have been trying to do or what forces we have sought to contain. And, he argues, it required the trauma of 9/11 to jolt Western political theorists into recognising both the anomalous status of their deeply held theories and the fragile nature of the institutions they had championed. At least in some of its forms, religion refused to depoliticise in the way modern liberal political theory requires it to be.

Of course, the religion/secular distinction was never in practice absolute, and the tensions that erupted post-9/11 simply made conspicuous and unavoidable a range of tensions which were always simmering beneath the surface. It forced us to recognise that the secular age was not what we had been taught. Lilla, himself an atheist, refers to the genealogies of Western secularism as the self-serving "fairy tales of our

---

[2] Of the significant body of literature demonstrating the invention of the modern concept of "religion," see especially Peter Harrison, *The Territories of Science and Religion* (Chicago, IL: University of Chicago Press, 2015) and Brent Nongbri, *Before Religion: The History of a Modern Concept* (New Haven, CT: Yale University Press, 2013).

[3] Mark Lilla, *The Stillborn God: Religion, Politics and the Modern West* (New York: Vintage, 2008), 308.

time."[4] A post-secular age had begun to force itself upon the consciousness of the West, an age in which religion would not go away.[5]

Much of the discourse and the practice around the church's community services was informed by the ideologies of modern political theory and the institutions of the state which evolved through the outworking of such theory. With this the case, we in the churches have participated in this three-hundred-year-long experiment. Yet, even as the limitations of the experiment become more obvious, we in the church find it very hard to let go of the religion/secular distinction. We are, as I will argue below, deeply enculturated into this form of politics, and it shapes how we understand the church's relationship with other institutions of the body politic.

In what follows, I will argue for a distinctly political view of Christianity which resists its relegation to the category of "religion." This view offers a particular self-understanding on the part of the church which includes within it an understanding of the place of the church in the world. I will sketch a way that Christians might articulate their understanding of and involvement in the matrix of power, economics, and decision making which characterise our present circumstance. Strictly speaking, this is more a theology of the church than a theology of community service agencies. Yet, it is a theology of the church which includes an understanding of the kinds of relationships with the world embodied in the agencies.

---

[4] Lilla, *The Stillborn God*, 311.
[5] On this, see Charles Taylor, *A Secular Age* (Cambridge, MA: Belknap, 2007).

It is important to state that the doing is *explicitly* theological work. From my participation as a theologian in the relevant discussions in the Uniting Church in Australia (UCA), the theological issue which keeps coming up is that of the nature of the church. Behind debates about funding, competition, contracts, identity, values, professionalization, and respective accountabilities to government and church lie deeper questions concerning the nature of the church. That theological issue drives this paper.

Against that background, the following is built around three relatively discrete theses which are then woven together in a concluding section. The four main sections of the paper are developed as follows:

1. Notwithstanding the resilience of the secular/religious distinction, cultural circumstances require us to accept that our context in Australia is post-secular.
2. Community services, isolated from the gathered community, cannot in any meaningful sense be considered the church.
3. The theology of the Uniting Church's *Basis of Union* is well placed to resource an ecclesiology suited to the post-secular context.
4. Weaving the above theses together allows us to sketch some possible relationships between gathered Christian communities and the church's community service agencies.

From the Secular/Religious Distinction to the Post-secular Context

Marion Maddox's examination of government funding of schools illustrates well the resilience of the secular/religious distinction. Many will be well aware of her arguments on this issue. She opposes public funding of "Christian schools" on the grounds that such funding is an abandonment of the century-long Australian project of a free, secular, and compulsory education. This leads her, negatively, to oppose the funding of "religious" schools and, positively, to "reclaim the secular," the title of the final chapter of her book, *Taking God to School*.[6]

Though this may seem somewhat tangential to the presenting issue of community service agencies, the church's involvement in education is not unrelated. At issue is not her critique of government funding of religious schools *per se*. There are all sorts of moral, philosophical, and cultural arguments, and even Christian theological arguments, which advance her position. The interest in Maddox is due to her well-honed concept of the secular/religious distinction. Her use of it demonstrates, albeit inadvertently, how conceptually blunt that distinction is as a tool; it lacks the necessary sharpness needed for policy formulation or cultural analysis our contemporary context demands.

Much of this bluntness stems from her attempt to transfer a set of concepts developed to address a particular nineteenth-century problematic into a quite different twentieth-century problematic. She rightly points out that the background to the free, secular, and compulsory public education system emerged as part of the project of nation building. Its founders believed that "[t]he new nation deserved nothing less than for all its children to enjoy the best education, side by side, and to grow up knowing that their destinies were bound

---

[6] Marion Maddox, *Taking God to School: The End of Australia's Egalitarian Education* (Sydney: Allen & Unwin, 2014).

together."[7] She further points out that the system's founders "thought that the segregated religious schools that preceded universal public education were damaging the colonies' social cohesion."[8]

All this is fair enough. For present purposes, the focus is her definition of the secular—that which she wants to reclaim. In debate with anti-secular arguments produced by some Christians, she notes that the definition of the "secular" as anti-God is itself a recent development.

> The idea that the secular must be "essentially anti-God" is very recent. The word "secular" derives from the Latin *saeculum*, meaning an age or a generation, and so in medieval usage came to refer to this world (where the ages roll on) as distinct from the things that pertain to eternity. It entered English first as an adjective to distinguish the "secular clergy" (who live in the world) from cloistered members of religious orders (who separate themselves from the world as far as possible). From there, it came to refer to other things related to the world outside the church, but not with any sense of opposition: in this medieval and early modern usage, people took a break from secular affairs to attend church religiously. There they heard sermons from secular clergy, and the church happily received the tithes from secular earnings. Other meanings accrued to the word over time—during the Reformation, "secularisation" referred to the seizing from monasteries by the crown, for example. The concept of secular education, meaning education in which religious doctrine does not form part of the subject matter, entered common usage in the nineteenth century. It did not, however, carry any automatic tone of anti-religion.[9]

---

[7] Maddox, *Taking God to School*, 31.
[8] Maddox, *Taking God to School*, 31.
[9] Maddox, *Taking God to School*, 201.

Maddox's potted history of the fluidity of the term "secular" is fine as far as it goes, as is her claim that "secular" does not *necessarily* mean *anti*-God. Nevertheless, jumping from the Reformation to the nineteenth century is problematic. It bypasses precisely the de-theologising of the secular and the de-politicising of religion that occurred during the development of modern political societies during that period. This causes her to overstate the neutrality towards religion implicit in the secular. To the extent that it is tolerant of religion, it is only so in the most minimal sense.

Yet perhaps the key issue with the distinction, as employed by Maddox, is the assumption that the secular will guarantee social cohesion. On what basis does this confidence rest? Is this an empirically provable claim? Should we discount the possibility that religious communities, precisely on the basis of their most fundamental *religious* convictions and doctrines—the very convictions and doctrines disqualified by the secular—do a better job at forming people who are committed practitioners of social cohesion? Indeed, one might speculate (and Maddox herself does point in this direction)[10] that nineteenth-century Christian religious leaders supported secular education precisely because of their shared Christian convictions about serving society.

What happens, however, when the religious diversity which secularism tries to control and contain is not just intra-Christian denominational diversity but the diversity of Christianity alongside other world religions? Can the concept of the secular actually produce social cohesion? This type of question is present in education but soon moves beyond it: nearly every political theorist working today observes that the

---

[10] See Maddox, *Taking God to School*, 52–55.

concept of the secular is a Western concept developed to solve a problem internal to Western Christendom. We should not assume that the idea of the secular can be easily transferred to cultures more religiously mixed than those of Western Christendom.

This point is made, perhaps as clearly as it can be, by Islamic political theorist Talal Asad in his *Formations of the Secular*.

> Islamism's preoccupation with state power is the result not of its commitment to [triumphalist or moralistic] ideas but of the modern nation-state's enforced [secular] claim to constitute legitimate social identities and arenas [e.g., religion]. No movement that aspires to more than mere belief or inconsequential talk in public can remain indifferent to state power in a secular world.[11]

To interpret Asad's argument: Islam's objection to secularism is not at base moralistic or triumphalist nationalism; it is Islam's principled assertion of the irreducibly public and political nature of its way of life. Islam does not fit the category of religion as defined by modern political theory. Nor, in my view, does Christianity.

So why is this distinction so resilient? Essentially, we have been enculturated into it. To borrow some words of Brad Gregory developed in another context: "Citizens are socialized into its assumptions as they pass through the various institutions of modern liberal societies."[12] And if we have been enculturated into the idea of the "secular," so we

---

[11] Talal Asad, *Formations of the Secular: Christianity, Islam, Modernity* (Stanford, CA: Stanford University Press, 2003), loc 3176–79 of 5724, Kindle.

[12] Brad Gregory, *The Unintended Reformation: How a Religious Revolution Secularized Society* (Cambridge, MA: Belknap, 2012), 386.

have been equally enculturated into the idea of "religion." The point is made by Craig Calhoun in *Re-thinking Secularism*:

> In all cases, secularism is defined in tandem with its twin concept, religion, and how we think about one of these paired concepts affects the way we think about the other. The rise of politically active religion not only encroaches on the supposed relationship between religion and secularism, thus challenging our thinking about the public role of religion, but it also queries our operative notions of secularism. The rise of politically active religious movements complicates our ideas about modern life—in particular, what many of us had regarded as its essentially secular character.[13]

Religion is not apolitical, and modern culture is not *de facto* secular. Rather than "reclaiming the secular," modern culture is today post-secular. We need to reclaim Christianity (and Islam, Hinduism, Judaism, etc.) from the category of "religion."

Community Services, Isolated from the Gathered Community, Cannot in Any Meaningful Sense Be Considered the Church

The reason for making this claim is to engage the counter-claim, i.e., that community services can replace the gathered community as the church. This idea, that community services can replace gathered communities, has been included by Keith Suter as one of four scenarios developed through his application of "scenario planning" to the future of the Uniting Church.[14]

---

[13] Craig Calhoun, *Rethinking Secularism* (Oxford: Oxford University Press, 2011), 6.

[14] Keith Suter, "Four Scenarios on the Future of the Uniting Church," *Uniting Church Studies* 20, no. 1 (2014): 1–21.

Suter himself has no particular commitment to this one approach; it is presented as an option to be considered. He also acknowledges that neither this nor any of the other three scenarios he explores were in conversation with either theological considerations or formal criteria. Though Suter may not himself advocate for this particular scenario, what he outlines is given voice from time to time in informal discussions concerning the future of the Uniting Church. This scenario is part of the conversation about the identity and future of the UCA.

Suter titles this approach "Secular Welfare." Though he intended to avoid theological categories he has, nonetheless, produced a scenario articulated entirely in the terms of the secular/religious distinction of modern liberal politics. Once again, we see the resilience of this particular distinction, our enculturation into this "norm," and the loss of a distinctly political view of the Christian community. Indeed, the concept of secular as it is used and implied in Suter's scenario is as hard a concept of secular as you could imagine. (To the extent that this does reflect some conversations in the Uniting Church, and if what I've argued in the previous section is sustained, it demonstrates that those conversations are significantly detached from current cultural circumstances.) Let's explore what he says.

In this scenario, Suter paints a picture of the UCA in which congregations and synods and presbyteries have been abolished. He writes:

> Freed from worrying about parishes/congregations, this Uniting Church will be able to move into new community service activities. It will not be weighed down with concerns about congregational matters. It will be able

to tender for government contracts without the risk of theological complications.[15]

The secularity of a secular vision of care could hardly be more explicit. It is not just that "theological complications" would be out of the way; so too would theological discourse *per se*. Or, to the put the matter a little differently, "deep discussions of religious belief" would be "evaded."

> This Secular Welfare scenario means that the recruitment of lay staff should become easier in that there is not the same search for Christian workers....This scenario means that UnitingCare can acknowledge its Christian heritage but not have any ambitions, reputation or facilities for evangelism. With the growing tide of humanitarian secularism, UnitingCare can evade deep discussions of religious belief.[16]

The reference here to the lack of any ambition, reputation, or facilities for evangelism is something of a furphy. The problem is deeper than simply not having "ambitions" for "evangelism" (whatever that might mean). By dissociating this proposal from all the negative connotations of evangelism, he obscures the more substantial implication of this scenario: UnitingCare would have no ambition, reputation, or facilities for discipleship formation, worship, or any intentional cultivation of Christian identity formed around the drama of Jesus risen and crucified. Above all, however, the real triumph of the secularity of this secular scenario lies here: "This scenario envisions a reduced prophetic role. This Uniting Church may have a caring heart but it will speak out less."[17]

---

[15] Suter, "Four Scenarios," 8.
[16] Suter, "Four Scenarios," 8.
[17] Suter, "Four Scenarios," 9.

And the explanation for this is perfectly logical: there would no longer be an intentional community of discipleship formation by which prophets would be produced and emerge. The theologically complicating drama of Jesus proclaiming the kingdom, being crucified and raised, the very drama which inspires, fosters, energises, and animates prophets and which is the foundation of a distinctly political view of Christianity would have been put to one side.

This would, in fact, constitute the complete capitulation by Christianity to the politics of the secular. Christianity would no longer be an embodied community but a set of values. This scenario envisages no role for gathered, organised, and mutually accountable Christian communities.

The reason to resist this scenario lies in the fact that intentional, gathered, worshipping Christian communities are essential for a Christian politics. Christianity does not become political by making prophetic statements—it is political in the most basic definition of that word by being a community which gathers people together around a shared way of life. And, of course, that shared way of life is called to be characterised as much by serving the world as by anything else. Christian politics is possible only through the existence of intentional, gathered, worshipping, and serving Christian communities.

In most of our UCA discourse we name such communities "congregations." The scenario outlined by Suter views "secular welfare" as the alternative to congregations. This is untenable. It is to be resisted not because of any romanticised view of congregations, or out of any nostalgia for their (alleged) hey-day, or from a commitment to any particular form of congregational life, or, least of all, out of any attempt to legitimate or perpetuate the well-documented dysfunctional features of many contemporary congregations. My resistance is driven by the simple conviction that without gathered communities of Christian people worshipping, witnessing, and serving there is no Christianity. If Christianity is reduced to "values," then it has ceased to be Christianity.

Lest this section be read as a preamble to denying any legitimacy to the agencies, let me stress the opposite. We can best develop a coherent ecclesiology which accommodates the orientation to service presently institutionalised in the agencies by first developing this distinctly political view of Christianity. Equally, lest this approach be thought of as isolating congregations from criticism, it would entail a radical transformation of our current understanding of the nature of a congregation.

The Theology of the Uniting Church's Basis of Union Is Well Placed to Resource an Ecclesiology Suited to the Post-secular Context

The *Basis of Union*[18] offers a combination of ecclesiology, eschatology, Christology, and history which, by definition, resists the modern categories of "secular" and "religion." The basic point is this: according to the Basis the church is not located in a sphere or a domain but in a universal and cosmic

---

[18] *The Basis of Union* is the document on which, during 1972 and 1973, the Presbyterian, Methodist, and Congregational Churches voted to unite in 1977 as the Uniting Church in Australia. According to the Constitution of the UCA, it remains the statement of the one, holy, catholic, and apostolic faith which is to guide the life and witness of the UCA. The text can be found in "Basis of Union," in *Theology for Pilgrims: Selected Theological Documents of the Uniting Church in Australia*, ed. Rob Bos and Geoff Thompson (Sydney, NSW: Uniting Church Press, 2008), 191–205.

history. In other words, instead of the church understanding itself and the world through largely spatial categories of "religion" and "secular," it is invited to understand itself through temporal categories: it is a community which exists and changes in history. While the church is presented as a particular body with a quite particular vocation, a vision of the church implied in the *Basis* can never quite know where to draw the lines between it and that which is not church. In fact, the lines are not just dotted lines; they are always being redrawn, and they can only ever be drawn faintly in the first place.

The view of the church in history as presented in §3 of the *Basis* represents a more classical theological sense of the "secular" prior to its modern spatial truncation. This age is defined as being the time between the events of Christ's death and resurrection and the final consummation: "The Church lives between the time of Christ's death and resurrection and the final consummation of all things which Christ will bring" (BoU, §3). This is not just time in some static purposeless sense; it is history open towards a particular goal. The *church* lives historically because *Jesus Christ* lives in this time. Not only does Jesus live, but in the midst of this time he *comes* to the church. As the *Basis* says, "Christ reaches out to command people's attention and awaken faith...; in his own strange way Christ constitutes, rules and renews them as his Church" (BoU, §4).

Within this framework, Christ cannot be configured by any categories, modern or otherwise. As during his earthly life, his strangeness eludes all such categories. Most of all, it eludes the category of "religion." Nor can Christ be contained or configured by the category of the "secular." Again, to return to §3: "Jesus is Lord over its own life;...Jesus is Head over all things, the beginning of a new creation, of a new humanity."

This is the lens through which we make theological sense of the much-quoted §11: "Within [the worldwide fellowship of churches] the Uniting Church also stands in relation to contemporary societies in ways which will help it to understand its own nature and mission." The openness to insights from beyond the church is not grounded in any particular virtue of the world; it is grounded, instead, in the conviction that Christ lives and rules there too.

What, though, of the almost just-as-frequently quoted comment about the congregation in §15? It is this claim which, perhaps more than any other, has been a point of contention in the discussions concerning the relationship between congregations and agencies. At face value, it appears to limit any extension of the "church" beyond the congregation. "The Congregation is the embodiment in one place of the One Holy Catholic and Apostolic Church, worshipping, witnessing and serving as a fellowship of the Spirit in Christ" (BoU, §15).

Does the reference to "one place" suggest a retreat to spatial and confined categories? No. Indeed, the real theological emphasis of this claim rests on the word "embodiment," with all its allusions to visibility and particularity. More than that, any spatial confining of place is immediately qualified by its imaging of congregation as a fellowship in the dynamic of the Spirit of Christ. The congregation is determined, not by its formal adherence to any inherited ecclesiastical definitions of "congregation," but by its own history in the history of Christ. Separated from that "fellowship of the Spirit in Christ," there would be no reason to think of it as the embodiment of the church.

Though the barest of sketches, it allows us to say this about the vision of the church invited by the *Basis*: *The church is a particular visible community with a dynamic identity and vocation.*

It lives in the history generated and sustained by Jesus Christ; it exists in order to bear witness to him in word and deed. Notwithstanding its very definite and particular centre, its edges are constantly diffused into Jesus Christ's own larger history.

So understood, the church will resist all demands that it occupy a "space" in social arrangements defined by the domains of "religious" and "secular." Those categories and the political theories which utilise them are no longer useful tools for either the description or analysis of contemporary Australian society. Not beholden to this categorization, the church can begin to think about the character of the kind of community it is called to be by exploring its role in the universal history of Christ. It is possible to ask afresh, "To what form of collective, organised embodied life is the church called?"

To formulate an answer to that question, let us turn to a recent study of Paul's understanding of grace. In *Paul and the Gift*, John Barclay draws attention to Paul's notion of the "incongruity of the Christ-gift, a gift given without regard to worth."[19] Christians have frequently sentimentalised the idea of grace and integrated it into all sorts of apolitical pieties. Barclay argues, however, that the very incongruity of grace allowed Paul to be politically inventive in the various communities he founded and nurtured; it allowed him, says Barclay, to "bypass and thus subvert pre-constituted systems of worth."[20] Paul's grace-constituted politics "disregards previous forms of symbolic capital and thus enables the creation of new communities whose norms are set by the Christ-gift itself."[21]

---

[19] John Barclay, *Paul and the Gift* (Grand Rapids, MI: Eerdmans, 2015), 5.
[20] Barclay, *Paul and the Gift*, 6.
[21] Barclay, *Paul and the Gift*, 6.

So, for Paul, "the nature of the gift was embodied and clarified in novel social experiments,"[22] specifically "in the form of norm- violating communities" which were characterised by living "at a diagonal to the normal taxonomies of value."[23]

What if we were to use this discourse to understand and develop our congregations? Communities grounded in the history or the gift of grace, unconfined by any imposed category of religion or secular, and theo-politically imagined: communities which embody novel social experiments; norm-violating communities which live at a diagonal to normal taxonomies of value. The theo-politics of grace is essentially a politics of this incongruous grace made known in Christ and his strange way.

Even if the discourse is different, this reading of Paul's politics of grace resonates with some important features of the vision of the church found in the *Basis of Union*. Moreover, it gives us language to talk about this vision in a post-secular world with a theo-political imagination.

Weaving the Themes Together

This final section sketches some possible ways of conceiving the relationship between the church and its agencies after extracting that relationship from the distorting and constraining categories of "religious" and "secular." These sketches develop not as concrete policy or structural proposals. They emerge from the theological considerations outlined above and according to the key principle that the church derives its identity and significance from its visible participation in Christ's

---

[22] Barclay, *Paul and the Gift*, 567.
[23] Barclay, *Paul and the Gift*, 567.

history of reconciliation. Specific and regulatory definitions of congregations and agencies will come and go, but the horizon before which we stand is that of the ongoing history of Jesus Christ. Once we are free of the religious/secular distinction, we are freed to think of what is and is not church in a far more differentiated way. That which is not church includes, of course, a vast array of institutions and forces which make up our social and political culture. It includes the state and the economy, national and multinational corporations, voluntary organisations and businesses. It is that multitude of relationships between the church and the state, the economy, corporations etc., which surface in discussions about the community service agencies' relationships to the gathered church. From this follows the discussions concerning funding, competition, contracts, identity, values, and respective accountabilities to government and church.

Three issues which arise from this ongoing discussion invite further reflection:

1. a common vocabulary for congregations and agencies;
2. a shared calling to a counter-politics;
3. a shared calling to covenantal relationships.

A Common Vocabulary for Congregations and Agencies

By resisting the religious/secular distinction and its conceptual controls, both congregations and agencies are invited to understand themselves within the ongoing history of Christ. Congregations are not in the business of "religion." Agencies are not in the business of "secular welfare," nor is their chief responsibility to the "welfare sector." The relationship of the two, by extension, could be explored and developed within the framework of their common calling and responsibilities within the history of Christ. On the one hand, by employing this explicitly theological language, both congregations and agencies would develop their self-understanding not first using language derived from empirically- and sociologically-particular discourses. On the other hand, because the history of Christ is more extensive than either "religion" or the "secular," this framework would provide greater flexibility in understanding the multiplicity of relationships between the church and the various organisations and structures which make up the social and political culture. Developing a common theological vocabulary for their respective self-understanding enhances the possibility for mutual understanding and mutual accountability.

A Shared Calling to a Counter-politics

If the framework of Christ's ongoing history is assumed, implications follow for the forms of life to which both congregations and agencies are called. Taking a cue from the engagement with John Barclay's reading of Paul, both agencies and congregations could understand themselves as embodying the politics of grace as norm-violating communities which are prepared, as necessary, to "disregard previous forms of symbolic capital." Congregations (of the UCA and most other mainline churches in Australia) have negligible, if any, widely recognised symbolic capital. Their symbolism is often that of nostalgia or institutional decline. This is likely to remain the case if their self-understanding is filtered through the lens of "religion." If congregations can hear the call to embody the politics of grace, then the opportunity exists to develop new symbolic capital. They could be communities which visibly embody, and are known to embody, the virtues of (among others) love, hope, forgiveness, and compassion as a genuine counter-politics operating "diagonal to the normal taxonomies of value."

The agencies (of UnitingCare and parallel church agencies) may be able to claim a persistent measure of such symbolic capital. Recognised, to varying degrees, to be an established part of the nation's network of welfare providers, their symbolic capital is arguably greater than that of congregations. Yet, this degree of symbolic capital, and its scale vis à vis that of congregations, cannot of itself be the basis for validating their work. Within this framework of Christ's ongoing history, the politics of the agencies should be measured by the same criterion: Are they "norm-violating, incongruous political experiments of grace"? Embedded as they are within the vast welfare sector, it is likely to be harder for agencies than it is for congregations to become embodiments of such politics. The flexibility for "novel social experiments" is likely to be restricted. Yet, this might well be the key mandate for church-based agencies in the welfare sector: to be the locus of such novel social experiments where the virtues of love, hope, forgiveness, and compassion are definitive, not only for the forms and location of service, but also for the internal structures of the agencies. Such a mandate is likely to assume greater importance as the welfare sector becomes increasingly privatised and corporatised. This places increased pressure on the relationship with congregations. How might that pressure be addressed? Answering that brings me to the third and last of the issues being considered in this section.

A Shared Calling to Covenantal Relationships

In the present context of the UCA, there is a particular dynamic at play in the relationship between congregations and agencies which needs to be acknowledged. There is nothing intrinsic about this dynamic. It is a function of the circumstances of contemporary Australian society. There is an imbalance in the respective degrees of scale. On the one hand, there is the large and expanding (institutional and economic) scale of community services. On the other hand, there is the small and declining scale of the congregations. This disparity of scale is a potent force in the relationships between congregations and agencies. In the face of this disparity of scale, both agencies and congregations are likely to experience multiple frustrations when understanding their mutual relationship. Whatever the kind of relationships that might be developed between congregations and agencies against this disparity of scale, they need to be informed by a novel politics of grace in the context.

Presently, these relationships are mediated through the administrative and institutional arrangements between UnitingCare and the councils of the UCA. The suggestion is this: rather than attempt to mediate those relationships through such arrangements, they could be developed through covenants between UnitingCare and the Councils of the Uniting Church, and, through them, the congregations. Covenantal relationships could be more open, more ad hoc, less structured, and less cumbersome than the present relationships. They would provide an opportunity for greater variety in relationships between particular agencies and particular congregations. They would honour the fact that neither congregations nor agencies are any longer what they were when the foundations were laid for the existing relationships. Covenantal relationships would allow relationships between congregations and agencies to be particular, local, and limited: indeed, they could be a means of developing novel local experiments in the politics of grace. (We might consider a parallel with the relationship between so-called parent churches and so-called mission churches during and after the missionary era. There comes a time when the former must let go of the administrative and institutional connections with the former in order to allow the latter genuine independence and for each to concentrate on their own responsibilities. As a result, new relationships—often precisely covenantal—can then be pursued between the two churches.[24]) Such experiments could be built around UnitingCare training congregational members as volunteers, educating congregations in social structures and trends, fostering internships and work experience for clusters of young adult members of congregations. Congregations could be host communities for chaplains working in agencies and be places of hospitality for other staff and clients of UnitingCare. Of course, many such activities already exist, but a covenantal framework would highlight them more than they are via the present high-level and often fraught administrative and institutional relationships. If the latter were to be replaced with local covenantal relationships, then the particular embodiments of the novel politics of grace could well become more determinative for the future of the relationship between UnitingCare and congregations.

This chapter began with reference to Mark Lilla and his description of politics in the West during recent centuries as both an experiment and an anomaly. Ultimately, he argues for persisting with the experiment and for keeping theology out of politics.2 This paper argues, by contrast, for a theo-politics for a post-secular age in which Christian politics is of its very nature a perennial experiment. The politics of the gathered church and its agencies is one part of that experiment. The UCA

---

[24] I owe the suggestion of this parallel to John Flett.

includes both theological and historical features which allow it to engage that experiment with conviction and enthusiasm.

Towards a Theology of Social Service: A Reflection Paper after the UnitingCare Australia Leaders Forum

Ji Zhang 张骥

The formation of Uniting Church in Australia (UCA) was the result of practical expressions of mission. In order to participate more faithfully in God's mission in the world, the churches that came into union acknowledged that none of them had responded to God's love with a full obedience and that unity of churches is required to witness the Christian faith in the world. The journey towards unity was a collective calling to "bear witness of that unity which is both Christ's gift and will for the Church" (BoU, §1).[1] In 2017, the UCA celebrated the fortieth year of its journey and the extraordinary growth of Uniting and UnitingCare and the establishment of a wide network of community services across Australia. The document that guides the theology of UnitingCare, *Faith Foundations*, sees the whole network as rooted in the UCA's post-denominational identity.[2] Subsequent references will take the form: (FF, p. 3). Community services, more broadly, are

---

[1] The text of the *Basis of Union* can be found in "Basis of Union," in *Theology for Pilgrims: Selected Theological Documents of the Uniting Church in Australia*, ed. Rob Bos and Geoff Thompson (Sydney, NSW: Uniting Church Press, 2008), 191–205. Subsequent references will take the form: (BoU, §1).

[2] See UnitingCare Australia's "Faith Foundations" (2000), https://www.unitingcare.org.au/images/about/000000_admin_UA_Faith_Foundations.pdf.

part of the universal church in the world, tracing their origin back to the apostolic traditions that shaped Christianity as a world religion.

In the years since its founding, the UCA is now but one of multiple stakeholders working towards a common good for civil society. The government provides the majority of the funding for social services and regulates them through a system of accreditation to control the quality of service delivery. The recent "consumer-directed" care model puts the choice of service into the hands of clients. Competition will naturally select economically sustainable providers who continue to operate in the future. While UnitingCare's mission statement describes its mandate as voicing "the Uniting Church's commitment" to social needs, the church-service relationship is no longer bilateral but multilateral. UnitingCare is accountable to at least three major stakeholders: the church, the people, and the government.

What is the parent-child relationship between the UCA and the UnitingCare network? This paper unpacks this church-service tension by way of theological reflection. By discerning a theology of social service within the context of UnitingCare network, it creates a dialogue between the two overlapping missions and leads to a discussion of the common good of God's mission.

The terms "the church" and "the service" acknowledge two networks: the Uniting Church congregation-based mission and the UnitingCare service-based mission. These are not separate missions. On the contrary, they are innately connected through God's mission in the world. By extension, community services are not undertaking a missionary service on behalf of the UCA; they connect the UCA to the community, to where the whole UCA is called to be. Being a "service-church" is a calling within our post-denominational identity exemplified in the *Basis of Union*. It is also our future partaking in God's becoming—to use a philosophical term—drawing the church and the service into the Spirit of God who reconciled the world to God's self in Christ Jesus.

The Church-Service Tension

The separation between the church and service is an identity problem for UnitingCare as a church agency and the Uniting Church as a whole. Reading *Faith Foundations*, the problem appears to have its roots in UCA's theology of salvation. Part A of *Faith Foundations* states that "[t]he church is a fellowship of the Holy Spirit under Christ, living as a pilgrim people, and moving towards the promised goal of salvation" (FF, p. 3). This theology of social service follows a traditional understanding of salvation found within the Protestant tradition. Following David Merritt's account of the Uniting Church, the *Faith Foundations* document spoke to an audience at the time when the concept of salvation was individualised and privatised.[3] This view further assumes that the church's mission is primarily about salvation. Within this doctrine of salvation, social service becomes a vehicle to extend the salvation offered by the church into the world.

The motif of salvation is seen in this further statement: "Engaging the Church with the world through community services provides us with opportunity to live out the Christian vision" (FF, p. 4). The underlying assumption is that the

---

[3] The author of *Faith Foundations* relied on David R. Merritt's *Understanding the Uniting Church in Australia*, 3rd ed. (Melbourne, VIC: Uniting Church Press, 1992).

church is the primary purpose of social service, whereas the totality of community services is secondary to the church's mission. This was true historically. It is not the defining motivation of service provision today. Herein is an ecclesial problem—how do we understand the nature and function of being church?

The assumption of this linear church-service relationship is a distinction between the sacred and the secular. In a traditional Christendom worldview, there is an essential difference between these two overlapping realms. By definition, the being of the church drives the becoming of the service. The division between the being and the becoming is not only operational but also ontological. Ontology is a philosophical term to understand how we perceive the world around us at the most fundamental level of irreducible realities: how we name, categorise, and accept the primary reason(s) of our existence.

In Western philosophy of the Platonic tradition, Being determines Becoming, but Becoming cannot reshape Being. In Christian theology, the doctrine of salvation is also one-directional, from the church to the world, not the other way around. In comparison, Eastern philosophy of the Chinese tradition sees the world as shaped by two cosmic forces, Yin and Yang. The myriad of things are born out of the dialectic tension between them. A mother not only gives birth to her children; the unfolding life of her children also enriches the mother's being. In other words, Becoming can also redefine Being.

The question, then, is whether the doctrine of salvation is the unchanging Being. Should it continue to be the first article of faith and the final goal of the church? The final chapter of *Basis of Union* states:

> The Uniting Church affirms that it belongs to the people of God on the way to the promised end. The Uniting Church prays that, through the gift of the Spirit, God will constantly correct that which is erroneous in its life, will bring it into deeper unity with other Churches, and will use its worship, witness and service to God's eternal glory through Jesus Christ the Lord. (BoU, §18)

In a multicultural Australia, can we still contend that the promised end is all about personal salvation? *Basis of Union* §18 would suggest that universal reconciliation is in fact our understanding of God's purpose for creation: God the Alpha and Omega, the Creator and the Consummator of all things, who gives and sustains life by the Holy Spirit and is glorified through the Son, Christ Jesus. The promised end is God's consummation of all things. This is our Becoming, and this Becoming will constantly reshape our Being.

Paul proclaims God as reconciling the world to himself through Christ and entrusting us with the message of reconciliation (2 Cor 5:19). The Uniting Church forefathers also saw ecclesial unity as the gift of the Spirit, one that would bring a deeper unity within the church itself, including the church and the service, with that unity also driving us "to seek special relationships with Churches in Asia and the Pacific" (BoU, §2).

The Chinese Daoist philosopher Zhuang Zi said that "[i]nner virtue enables outer ruling." To put that in Christian theological terms—to reconcile the world, you first have to live out that reconciliation yourself. The capacity for seeking external relationships in the world derives from our inner unity and confidence of being in relationship with one another.

The separation between the church and the service is a relationship problem that requires a relational solution.

Within the breadth of the UCA, the community of faith is not limited to congregations of worshippers. Our journey of reconciliation is open to all the people of God within God's boundless love. This journey towards unity is not a mere product of human activity. In fact, the Spirit of God is there on the journey.

"God will constantly correct that which is erroneous in its life" for that promised end of reconciliation (BoU, §18). The division between church and service is just that—something erroneous in the life of UCA that the Spirit is calling us to correct. We cannot neglect mutual engagement if we are going to live out the spirit of reconciliation.

To be sure, the Uniting Church never sees its post-denominational identity as a fixed Being. The journey of the Uniting Church as God's pilgrim people is a process of Becoming. Our future will inevitably involve both the church and the service. The task of defining a theology of social service is to uphold the tension between them and create dialogues in preparation for our journey of reconciliation into the next forty years.

God's Mission from the Margins

To bring the church and the service together requires a theological dialogue that enables a relational conversation to take place. This dialogue begins with the acknowledgment that something has fundamentally changed for both the church and the service in the last forty years.

The confidence about personal salvation reflected the majority mind-set of the 1970's church. At that time, the church occupied the centre of society in the nation-state. This was a continuation of the history of Christendom with the state entering a period of prolonged growth and with Christianity prevailing as the state religion. Today, the church lies at the margins in a secular society. Christendom has ended in Australia, and our congregation-based ministry has declined.

According to the census statistics dealing with religious affiliation in Australia between the 2011 and 2016, while the Anglican Church has the biggest decline in terms of membership numbers, the Uniting Church has the largest decline by percentage (-18%).[4] In real terms, an average UCA congregation has as many members as a school classroom. Historical trends suggest that people are turning away from the institutional church. Yet the biggest growth is among culturally and linguistically diverse communities (CALD). According to National Church Life Survey, the cultural and ethnic make-up of Australian church congregations is increasingly diverse, with a third of churchgoers born overseas.[5] Faith is rediscovered in cultural diversity and social margins.

This reflects a paradigm shift from "Church's mission to the margins" to "God's mission in the margins." In a post-Christendom world, God is moving from the centre to the margins. Three assembly presidents have collectively pointed to this common theme: our being is in this God's becoming.

---

[4] The data was presented to the UnitingCare Leaders Forum in 2017 by Bernard Salt, https://gallery.mailchimp.com/31e263e0c9917f3f73933fcff/files/7ed4978f-e4bd-4fa4-b75b-3711b91129c5/172010_Presentations_Leaders_Forum.pdf.

[5] The survey is conducted every five years and collects data from more than 280,000 church attendees. The proportion of attendants born overseas was 28 percent in 2006 and reached 36 percent in 2016. See Hemangini Patel, "Christianity's Increasingly Multicultural Face Revealed in Australian Church Survey," 4 October 2017, http://mobile.abc.net.au/news/2017-10-04/is-multiculturalism-the-new-face-of-australian-church-life/9010714?pfmredir=sm.

"Our church is in Exile," the twelfth president of the UCA, Alistair Macrae, observed at his 2009 induction service. In the preamble debate, we saw God was moving from the centre to the margins. Like the incarnation, the Spirit of God has entered into this historical margin and called the church to wrestle with our alienation from the First Peoples in this land.

After attending the World Council of Churches (2013) and Christian Conference of Asia (2015), the thirteenth president, Andrew Dutney, reflected on the rising of minority churches in our Asia-Pacific region. He affirmed that "God is changing us in a powerful way." Like the rising of the crucified Lord, the passion narrative of Jesus has been re-enacted again and again in the growth of Christianity worldwide.

"The church is all about making an impact—not merely surviving." The fourteenth president, Stuart McMillan, spoke of hope after his return from the Middle East (2016). In the midst of an overwhelming influx of refugees, the churches worked together to assist the stranger and so to impact wider society. Like the early church, the contemporary church is a community of faith that exemplifies "God is hope."

The Uniting Church is in the global South. We are among a new centre of Christianity in the Asia-Pacific. In 1910, when the modern ecumenical movement came together in Edinburgh, 80 percent of the Christian population were in the global North. In 2010, 64 percent of the Christian population were found in the global South. The growth of Christianity is unprecedented. For instance, the Indonesian Communion of Churches has eighty-nine Protestant churches, representing 10 percent of the Indonesian population. The China Christian Council has grown from less than 1 million to 40 million in the last thirty years. By comparison, membership within the UCA is in numerical decline. Unlike the majority status it enjoyed in the past, it now represents only a single-digit percentage of the population.

Australia is becoming increasingly like our international partners: a society made up of culturally diverse and religiously plural peoples. Our growing ministries have emerged from multicultural and interfaith communities. Our community services have a large footprint throughout Australia because they entered the social margins where injustice and inequality cry out for compassion and care. To be sure, all such contexts are not only on the social margins but also on the margins of faith. In the past, the UCA lived in the paradigm of bringing the church's mission to the margins; today the church is called to receive God's mission from the margins.

Being not only gives birth to Becoming; Becoming will also reshape Being. Throughout the vast network of UnitingCare services, the Spirit of God is calling a new form of church into existence. This is not driven by evangelism, but woven together by relationships. It is not limited to one hour of worship on a Sunday morning, but open daily to people seeking support. While a large percentage of congregations are in decline, looking inward, and surviving on property incomes, our services have grown into a network of human relationships, reaching out to 1 in 12 Australians from all walks of life regardless of their cultural and religious background. This is a discourse of Becoming.

Our future is incarnational—to embody the gospel in the community. The question is why the missiology should reinvent the wheel. Over the past decades, this network of relationships has taken the church into the public, engaged the government, connected to communities, and responded to the needs of the most vulnerable. The church is called to reflect

God's mission from the margins, while allowing the service to reshape the church.

The Common Ground of Suffering

If we look into all services, and reflect truthfully, we see one thing in common—suffering. No matter how big or small, in city or country, delivering personal care or building communities, all services address the brokenness of the world. The common ground—the church, the government, the community, and the people—is the irreducible reality of human suffering. If we still think from the framework of Christian salvation, then the reality of suffering is the context within which the salvation preached by Jesus should be read and reinterpreted. More important, this common ground in suffering is, paradoxically, also the common good. Compassion towards suffering is the common good that all stakeholders share. The art lies in bringing all these stakeholders into common service. It will gather the collective hope of the people and available social resources and channel them towards a social discourse concerned with the relief of suffering through compassion and care.

All religions must face suffering as the irreducible problem of the world. Christianity as a religion cannot avoid the question of whether our theology and praxis answer the problem of suffering in changing circumstances.[6] Atonement theology believes suffering is related to the original sin of

---

[6] Douglas John Hall famously put forward two insights that suffering is a problem for God and a problem in creation. See Douglas John Hall, *God and Human Suffering: An Exercise in the Theology of the Cross* (Minneapolis, MN: Augsburg Press, 1986).

humanity. This account requires the substitutional atonement of Christ to bring salvation from the otherworldly God. It reduces suffering into morality, and theology dwells on a threefold moral restoration of "creation, fall, redemption." Instead of looking into suffering, it looks outward towards a transcendental deity for saving the soul. Modern liberation theology has challenged this otherworldly salvation of the soul and argued for the liberation of the embodied life, its liberation from social sins in this world. Feminist theology has taught us that our bodily experience of suffering is a source of theology.[7]

In a world of religious pluralism, theology no longer draws inspiration from a single source of doctrinal theology but rather dialogues with other faith traditions to broaden our horizon. Comparative theology teaches us that, unlike the Christian faith's concern with salvation, the first article of faith in Eastern religions, Buddhism in particular, is the doctrine of suffering. This insight leads us back to the biblical text, and here we rediscover a simple truth: without the cross there is no resurrection. The understanding of suffering is a gateway to transformation.

"The Son of Man does not come to be served but to serve, and give his life as a ransom for many" (Mark 10:45). The divinity of Christ is most profoundly revealed in the humanity of Jesus. When he was on his knees and washed the disciples' feet, the love of God united the disciples without words but by action (John 13:1-7). In John's Gospel, this is the middle point between the coming down of the Son of God (the incarnation of God) and the lifting up of the Son of Man (the glorification

---

[7] Robin Ryan presents an excellent theological survey on various answers to the problem of suffering. See Robin Ryan, *God and the Mystery of Human Suffering: A Theological Conversation Across the Ages* (New York: Paulist Press, 2011).

of God). Paul revealed the secret of Christ suffering when he said that "Christ emptied himself, taking the form of a slave, being born in human likeness" (Phil 2:7). To be of the same mind, having the same love, is essentially to learn from Christ. It is to be "in Christ." By Christ emptying himself into others, God gathers them into God's love and gives them rest.

On the cross, Jesus' suffering draws the world's attention to the irreducible problem of human suffering. He was tortured, bled, and died as the Son of God (Luke 22:42). This is the ultimate witness of God with us, in our deepest suffering when death strips all down to the raw emotion of being rejected and forsaken. Only by taking the suffering upon himself and being rejected by the world does Jesus open a pathway for all people to relate to God's love. When his arms are forced open by the nails, the Spirit is also holding together the Father and the Son in pain. God's anguish was shown through the temple curtains being torn from the top down (Mark 15:38). Luther names this suffering Christ the crucified God. Using Luther's provocative title, Moltmann turned the Neoplatonist dogma that God cannot suffer into a doctrine of Trinitarian community of suffering and hope.[8]

The church and the service stand together at the foot of the cross. Here is where the lonely and the most vulnerable are gathered before Jesus. The UCA president Stuart McMillan reminds us that our service network is where Jesus meets the most vulnerable. Their loneliness is a reverse image of our celebrated individualism. Their raw emotion of brokenness overlooks the institutional structure of the church and seeks pastoral care regardless of denominational difference. Their feelings of being rejected by family, community, or country

---

[8] Jürgen Moltmann, *The Crucified God* (London: SCM, 1974).

draw out people's compassion for life. Their needs which result from ageing call into question the material happiness promised by modern consumerism and demonstrate the importance of emotional care.

All these people want compassion. The people in the margins resonate with the crucified Jesus. For Christians, the cross is also about life. The church and the service offer companionship to people feeling forgotten by the world.

The service is not one-way. Within the UCA, sometimes the needy also want to care and to give. Some volunteers are poor but generous and compassionate towards others. Indeed, Christ both suffers and gives, cares. Even if we are called to companion others in our community in need, we are not only carers—we also experience need. As the church we too receive something through sharing in the life situation of others. In this way, the church is further connected with communities through the service.

Looking through the cross, we see this Spirit is calling a new church into existence. Jesus' passion narrative has been re-enacted again and again through community services—in the fringes of society as well as in the margins of faith. Instead of bringing people into the confined walls of church buildings through the gate of confession, God's mission drives both the church and the service into the wildernesses of Australia to be tested by the Spirit. And the same Spirit is about to renew both the church and the service by gathering communities together under the cross—to be embraced by God's love. This coming together of the church and the service will shape a new crucible of life in which the indigenisation of the Uniting Church is being made.

Service-Church Is the People of God

Instead of seeing the service as part of the church, here we begin to see that "the service is the church." This hypothesis shifts theological reflection away from "what the church does" through community services towards "what the church is" in a network of relationships. This reflection process not only reverses the order of doctrinal theology from Being to Becoming but also creates a dialogue from Becoming to Being. The following considers this shift through three formal theological images of the church:

- the People of God,
- the Creation of the Spirit,
- and the Body of Christ.[9]

The origin of the church was simply a gathering of the people. A core group of disciples were called to act in anticipation of the immediate arrival of the kingdom of God. Then Jesus' followers gathered as a community of hope; they heard his teachings and witnessed his healings. Although most of his followers left Jesus when he was put to death, they were gathered again by the spirit of his resurrection.

On the day of Pentecost, the coming of the Spirit radically shook up this small Jewish community named the "Jesus sect." The Spirit of God called the people of God into a new existence by enabling those who had different cultural and linguistic backgrounds to speak praises to the Spirit of life that came into their shattered communities. Then the church was formed

---

[9] Here I borrow from Hans Küng's description of the threefold attributes of the church, without following his wider ecclesiology. Hans Küng, *The Church* (New York: Sheed & Ward, 1967), 107–260.

and a gentile Christianity developed. God's gracious act in Jesus Christ overcame the distinction between the Jews and the gentiles in this vision of God's kingdom. Those who were once outsiders had become insiders.

Among many discussions on the ecclesial identity of the service, there is one often misinterpreted quote within the *Basis of Union*:[10] "The congregation is the embodiment in one place of the One, Holy, Catholic and Apostolic Church, worshipping, witnessing and serving as a fellowship of the Spirit in Christ" (BoU, §15a). Some people assume the threefold attributes of "worship, witness, and service" provide the criteria of being a church. To be clear, the claim "the service is the church" does not question the importance of the congregation within the structure of the Uniting Church, although the argument requires that all UCA congregations be measured by these three attributes. It does affirm, however, that God's mission is one. The UCA does not have two separate missions—one which belongs to the church and one which guides the service. On the contrary, God's mission is calling the service-church into existence. And we need to come to terms with what God's mission is today.

Within the diversity of the UCA, God's mission is inclusive of congregational ministries, community services, Congress, and other agencies. "All of these are us." This theme from the celebration of the UCA's fortieth year highlights the mutually inclusive nature of our post-denominational journey. The first theological title, "the People of God," calls us to look deeper

---

[10] In my various conversations with congregational ministers and interviews with church leaders, I have heard a common perception. It sees congregational ministry as the core existence and quotes the *Basis of Union* as the foundation while overlooking inner connection between two ministries within the whole UCA.

into the reality of where the church is among the people today. "For where two or three are gathered in my name, I am there among them" (Matt 18:20). The church is where Christ meets people. Community services have established community-to-community connections, embodying the church and the service relationships through solidarity with the poor, the marginalised, the voiceless, the vulnerable, and the fallen. The scope of "the People of God" has to be broadened to include a range of communities. This brings God's mission into focus. God makes the outsider the insider while dissolving the distinction between faith and action. Loving one's neighbour is a valid path for loving God.

UCA General Secretary Colleen Geyer reminds us that the mission and the operation of the business are not two distinctive parts of one organisation. Instead, a definition of mission for faith-based community service has to return to the purpose of our shared existence—the people. We are called to care for the people. Under this overarching mission, other operational parts of an organisation become integrated expressions of God's mission.[11] A recent study by *Uniting Vic.Tas* points towards a trend where mutual engagement between congregations and community services become a priority of mission.[12] Many congregations are unaware that the service is trying to build a culture where it is seen as part of the church.

The Uniting Church is not just the one but also the many. The *Basis of Union* maintains that "one Spirit has endowed the

---

[11] Colleen Geyer, "Transforming Mission in Faith–Based Community Services," *Uniting Theology and Church*, no. 3 (2010): 6–9.
[12] Martin J. Cowling, "Toward a Model of Mutual Engagement: Community Programs across the Uniting Church in Tasmania and Victoria," Unpublished Discussion Paper, 19–20.

members of Christ's Church with a diversity of gifts, and that there is no gift without its corresponding service: all ministries have a part in the ministry of Christ" (BoU, §13). To be "People of God" means becoming and being "a fellowship of the Spirit in Christ." Building Australian communities requires more than the church. Indeed, it requires the service-church to bring different skills and equip people with a diversity of gifts into corresponding service. Community services have developed this comprehensive capability on behalf of the whole UCA. These gifted people have taken responsibility for providing services where there is overlapping social, cultural, political, economic, as well as religious interests. The people are the common good.

What might happen if we think of "worship, witness, and service" not as marks of the church, but as three functions, indicating *what the church does* but not *what the church is*? The *Basis of Union* rightly points out that God "will use" these functions for God's mission. We can find two paragraphs where all three terms are jointly used (BoU, §§1, 18). The UCA's founding document begins and ends with the church's humble submission to Christ. God will use "what church does" as the vehicle to show "what the church is"—God has reconciled the world to God's self through Christ Jesus (2 Cor 5:19).

Service-church is the People of God. The assertion speaks for the communion of God and the people. In the early church, the Spirit of Pentecost brought the enclosed community of Israel back to its original meaning—the reign of God united the twelve tribes and transformed the exclusive identity of Israel into an inclusive community of many gentiles. Today, the dialogue between the church and the service reopens that ancient debate. In fact, it returns the mission of the church back to the mission of God, to God with us. The active participation of social service in the life of all people keeps the door of the UCA open to the world. The service-church influences social policies to uphold social values and civic virtues "so that ethical governance and moral practice distinguish all corporate decision-making." The most effective advocacy is done through relationships with the government for the people.

In the early church, the People of God fixed their gaze upon the messianic hope that "God will dwell with the people" (Ezek 37:27; Rev 21:3). Today, this hope is still transforming a local people into a future-oriented community; all the faithful belong to the People of God.

During the debate surrounding the revised preamble to its constitution, the UCA learned to honour God who was in this land prior to the missionaries' arrival.[13] The implication of this historic recognition is yet to be fully felt in Australian society. It implies that God not only dwells with the First Peoples in this land but also makes God's own dwellings in this ancient land among all people, including culturally and linguistically diverse communities. This is a radically inclusive community; everyone who calls on the name of the Lord will be delivered (Joel 2:32; Rom 10:13). This mystery was present when the First Peoples began to call on the name of the Lord in their journey of faith and is now present as they continue to struggle for identity in the land.

The old debate about the insider and the outsider is no longer relevant. To be with the people is God's own choosing—God with us. The task of theology also changes

---

[13] The text of the revised preamble is available here: https://assembly.uca.org.au/images/stories/covenanting/PreamblePoster-web.pdf.

because theology recognizes this pre-missionary God and evokes the pre-existing messianic hope—in this ancient land—embracing all people.

Service-Church Is the Creation of the Spirit

The creation of new life begins on the cross, in and through which God reveals God's self to be God with us, even in suffering. The trinitarian community of life helps explain such a mystery.1[14] On the cross, the interconnected life of the Trinity was torn apart in the cry that Jesus was forsaken by the Father (Ps 22; Mark 15:34; Matt 27:46). In that same moment, the Spirit held the Father and the Son in the pain of divine love. The cross is a paradox of suffering and of life. The separation between the Father and the Son opens the inner trinitarian life to the world.

At the cross there is a perpetual opening of the Triune God. Whoever is willing to come before this open Trinity will be embraced by the crucified God. At the shadow of the cross, we hear the voice: "This man truly was the Son of God!" (Mark 15:39). Looking from the other side of the cross, God's everlasting compassion for all people is disclosed and stretched into four cardinal directions. "For God so loved the world that he gave his only Son, so that everyone who believes in him may not perish but may have eternal life" (John 3:16).

---

[14] Moltmann and Volf have separately argued the central connection between God and the church that views the church as both the image of, and empowered by, the trinitarian life of God. Jürgen Moltmann, *The Church in the Power of the Spirit* (Minneapolis, MN: Fortress Press, 1993); Miroslav Volf, *After Our Likeness: The Church as the Image of the Trinity* (Grand Rapids, MI: Eerdmans, 1998).

Service-church is the creation of the Spirit. Empowered by the resurrection of Christ, its mission is about the rising of the fallen. It is open to whoever is willing to be touched by the Spirit of life and to join the movement to say yes to life and no to death. Like the creation of life at the beginning of the world, the resurrection of Christ is the creation of life out of nothing. In the midst of public despair, God raises Jesus to life. By the spirit of resurrection, a theology of service turns our views of human nature back to the origin of humanity. Being created in the *imago Dei* (image of God) means that human beings are created equal. This intrinsic value within each human being is not tarnished by any life circumstances. It is a created order that can only be given but not removed. This dignity is to be restored and not forgotten.

Service-church as the creation of the Spirit brings hope to the world by extending the resurrection of Christ to the restoration of humanity. Such a confidence in God's grace can be traced to the Reformation. The doctrine of justification by faith rests on God's saving grace. Justification also includes sanctification of people. Our community services continue this tradition by working collectively in the sanctification of the First and Second Peoples. It affirms the universal personhood of all people by affirming their equality—"Everyone has the right to receive care." This operating philosophy of UnitingCare carries the resurrection motif of the crucified Christ. God's answer to suffering does not bypass death but enters into its deepest agony in the death of the Son. God's justice lets the fullness of life be the answer to multifaceted suffering.

The acts of care and service gather new communities and form relationships from small drop-in centres to large hospitals and aged care centres. All these services extend

God's mission of life by forming life-giving relationships of care with individuals and building resilient communities through community development. All these relationships are part of the UCA. For the church to fully take ownership of community services we need a fuller doctrine of the Spirit, one that articulates the interconnected life between the Spirit of God in Christ and the spirit of life among the people.[15]

Forty years ago, when the UCA was formed as the post-denominational church, the people acknowledged that none of the three preceding denominations "has responded to God's love with a full obedience" (BoU, §1). Subsequently, unity was achieved through the reconciliation built on the foundation of Christ (BoU, §2). Having journeyed forty years, the UCA is still called into interconnected relationship. In 2017, the Assembly Standing Committee passed the Assembly Strategic Plan. At its core, this plan seeks to discern God's mission in order to renew us through a relational model of collaboration among four councils of the church.

Moltmann once was asked, "What is the difference between an NGO and Church-based service?" His answer was simple: "Whether or not Christ is witnessed." His answer, of course, is much broader than a simple confession of Jesus as our Lord and personal saviour. Within his broad theological scope, witness is about whether the historical Jesus is relived through the empowerment of the poor, healing of the sick, the raising

---

[15] The doctrine of the Spirit is a weak field in Protestant theology. In the world dominated by scientific truth and rational thinking, the discussion of the Spirit reminds the church that Christianity is a religion and that its teachings are based not on rational ethics but on the transformative hope for new life in communities. Jürgen Moltmann, *The Spirit of life: A Universal Affirmation* (Minneapolis, MN: Fortress Press, 1992).

up of the humiliated.[16] More important, the cosmic Christ is evident in the new creation when human beings are reconciled with each other and with God's creation.[17] We are called to witness to hope.

We need a relational ontology.[18] The Trinity is both the one and the many. The inner life of the Trinity unfolds into the economy of God's creation. Within the trinitarian life, the unity of God is achieved through mutual participation of three Persons in life-giving relationships. When the inner life of the Trinity unfolds into the world, it calls the church to partake in God's economy of life by forming relationships that enable mutual participation. This relational ontology among three Persons provides the base of interconnectedness in our relationship with each other. One Person can find the true self only in the relationship with others in the divine community. Within the Trinity, the unity of the divine community and the diversity of each Person can be either both affirmed or simultaneously rejected.

Mutual relationship is a two-way path of giving and receiving. In the doctrine of the Trinity, there is no determination of the "one over many." At the heart of tri-unity there is only the mutual indwelling of the "one within many."[19] This is a relationship of interdependency by the act of mutually giving

---

[16] Jürgen Moltmann, *The Way of Jesus Christ: Christology in Messianic Dimensions* (London: SCM, 1990), 94–116.

[17] Moltmann, *The Way of Jesus Christ*, 274–312.

[18] I have developed this idea in my book based on a comparative study between two ancient traditions. Ji Zhang, *One and Many: A Comparative Study of Plato's Philosophy and Daoism Represented by Ge Hong* (Honolulu: University of Hawaii Press, 2012).

[19] My account of this relational ontology is more fully articulated in Ji Zhang, "A Trinitarian Theology of Multiculturalism," *Uniting Church Studies* 18 (2012): 47–58.

and receiving life from each other. Within each person's inner being, there is a self-emptied space, created to give room for the other to exist. Augustine once called this sacred space "divine love." The Daoist philosopher Ge Hong named it the "chamber of Qi." It is the same life that connects the microcosm of the body with the macrocosm of the universe.

Service-church breathes through this life of God. Both the church and the service create self-emptying rooms for the Spirit of life to interpenetrate both. The creation of the Spirit affirms the freedom to be in relationship, with individuality not swallowed by the other. Paul reminds us that "where the spirit of the Lord is, there is freedom" (2 Cor 2:17). This freedom of being in relationship can no longer be categorised as the church's salvation in the world or doing service on behalf of the church. Instead, this very act of being in relationship is where the Spirit of life dwells. "When the Spirit comes, it will guide you into all truth" (John 16:13). The Spirit of life will set us free from the weight of old assumptions and point to a path leading to all truth. It draws the church and the service together in dialogue, creates space for mutual indwelling, and moves both into God's outpouring Spirit. In such a way, the UCA partakes in the economy of God.

Living in the economy of God empowers the UCA to advocate for life in Australian society. Christian faith derives from "the resurrection of the body" as defined by the Nicene Creed. A new life in God means affirming life against death. The Spirit of resurrection urges Christians to advocate for the quality of life in every person's bodily existence. In this way, the Good News in Jesus might be exemplified in the society and become the lived experience for people here and now. Life also includes death. In residential care, we can learn from our palliative care staff what a good death means for the dying and the family.

Since its formation, UnitingCare Australia has been acting cooperatively to care for the vulnerable, to bring healing to broken relationships, and to "sustain the fragile networks that are essential for the maintenance of the Common Good" (FF, §2.4). This list summarises some enduring values:

- Equality: Each person is equal regardless of personal attributes
- Justice: Every person has the right to fully participate in the civil society
- Empowerment: Partake in democratic decision making to empower people
- Embodiment: Embody the love of God in the world
- Quality: Promote best practice in service delivery
- Advocacy: Speak for the most disadvantaged in society
- Innovation: Undertake research to develop policy and influence outcomes
- Relationship: Build a collaborative network to exemplify God's reconciliation[20]

These values represent the shared interests of multiple stakeholders. Instead of extending salvation from the church to the world, the creation of the Spirit works in the area where life brings in all stakeholders, all who together explore and establish healthy and life-giving relationships in the shalom of God. Creating relationships enables the whole community service sector to work towards a common goal. This is a mission of the service-church.

---

[20] The list of core values is a summary of "Faith Foundations," Part A.

Service-Church Is the Body of Christ

The process of discerning the mission of service-church will move our focus from "the church's mission to the margins" to "God's mission from the margins." This lesson was learned in the context of international relationship. At the fourteenth UCA assembly held in Perth, Prof. Lin Manhong, associate general secretary of China Christian Council (CCC), delivered the Cato Lecture.[21] Her speech, "To Be a Marginal People of God," called for a transition from a majority mind-set to a minority insight.

UnitingCare has been supporting the Chinese church in leadership training for four years. In that engagement, we have learned that social service grows out of the changed life of individuals. Where public preaching is not allowed, Christian witness takes the form of living out God's love without words but by action. "For the Son of Man came not to be served but to serve, and to give his life a ransom for many" (Mark 10:45). Learning from Christ, these Christians provide service in very humble circumstances without seeking a return. As a social minority, they read the gospel from the marginal perspective. As Jesus himself put it, "Foxes have holes, and birds of the air have nests, but the Son of Man has nowhere to lay his head" (Matt 8:20). Their witness adopts a form of journeying with the most vulnerable and caring for the least and the forgotten. And they practice the biblical teaching that "faith without works is dead" (Jas 2:14). Service provision is itself an act of worshipping God. Community services provide multiple pathways for church growth.

---

[21] Lin Manhong, "Cato Lecture – Living on the Margins," *Crosslight*, no. 258 (2015): 18.

As one example, there is an HIV clinic in the ancient capital, Xian. It was started by a group of old ladies in a house church. They looked after the dying in their neighbourhood and debated with church leaders on God's unconditional love towards the people living with AIDS. They were questioned by the local church regarding the moral teaching on sins and redemption, but they gained support from the central government, the national church, and the Bill Gates Foundation. Last year, this small clinic mobilised two thousand university students as volunteers. As the young people visited gay gatherings and offered tests to sex workers, they became advocates for awareness and change. This ministry of the laity has taken the church to the margins of society, indeed to the margins of Christian faith. But it has equally expended public space for the minority faith. Now the provincial synod has reorganised the clinic and the house church next door so that together they are a congregation.

The story reminds us of the minority nature of service-church. Standing in the social margins, we can see a deeper connection between God and God's mission. Theologically, the church does not have a mission, but the mission of God calls the church into being.

Missio Dei > Missio ad gentes + Missio inter gentes

The mission of God is bigger than the simple combination of the "mission to the gentiles" and the "mission with the gentiles." In mission with the gentiles, the horizon of God's mission begins to open and brings the common interest between the church and the service into focus—life.

God's mission is not limited to the "mission *to* the gentiles." The creation of the Spirit moves the whole church to do "mission *with* the gentiles" to achieve the common good.[22] "Mission *to* the gentiles" sees the world as the secular "other," contrary to its own sacred tradition. "Mission *with* the gentiles" opens the horizon of mission, creating multiple opportunities within public space for the UCA to renew its mission in the fellowship of the Spirit of life.

Service-church is the Body of Christ. It is in and through the service that Christ's crucified yet risen life can be embodied among the marginalised. The task of the church is to name God in this self-emptying act of enhancing life. This outward sending forth of God's self is the continual incarnation of God's own life in the world—regardless of the church's capacity to conceptualise its fullness in theology.

At the heart of service-church is the incarnation. The life of God unfolds into the world, not with power, but with a perpetual presentation of a newborn life. Matthew's Gospel tells us, "for the child conceived in her is from the Holy Spirit" (Matt 1:20). It indicates that the Spirit of God was infused in the life of Jesus. The Nicene Creed affirms the personhood of Jesus was "conceived by the Holy Spirit, and born of Virgin Mary." In the Hebrew context, the birth of Christ was believed to be God's fulfilment of ancient prophecy, the people should call the child Immanuel: "God is with us." In dialogue with Hellenistic tradition, John went a step further, proclaiming that the pre-existing Logos of the universe had taken on human flesh.

"The Word became flesh" is translated into the Chinese language as "the Dao has become/completed the flesh body

---

[22] The distinction was first conceptualised through UnitingCare training in China. To be in dialogue with the government is an important aspect of the partnership. It helps increase the level and footprint of leadership capacity building in church-based aged care facilities.

道成了肉身" (John 1:14). This extraordinary claim can be understood only in terms of interfaith dialogue between the doctrine of the Trinity and Daoist soteriology. The life of God, which created the whole universe, proceeds through the Spirit and is emptying God's self to bring the flesh-body to its fullness. The beginning of the infant life of Jesus signals the ending of our search for immortal life. Each person can live to the fullness of that natural endowment—"the Dao has become/completed flesh"—in the world.

To be a service-church is to be Christ's body in the world. Such a church is not limited by the membership of baptised people; it incarnates its existence like salt and light in its life-preserving relationship with people in need. Recently, the World Council of Churches held a forum on churches working ecumenically on social service. Ecumenical *diakonia* (Greek term for "service") means complementing each other in what we do best: serving our local communities. This service helps bring visible church unity to the world. In the UnitingCare network, ecumenical cooperation has been practiced for many years. "For in the one Spirit we were all baptized into one body—Jews or Greeks, slaves or free—and we were all made to drink of one Spirit" (1 Cor 12:13). What is new, however, is that within community services this ecumenical cooperation needs to be intentionally claimed as part the of ecumenical identity of the Uniting Church.

To be a service-church is to be an inclusive Body of Christ in the world. We are salt and light in the world, seeking to be catalysts of God's abundant love. Salt must dissolve in order to preserve food. Likewise, the church must move into society in order to be tasted for its saltiness. As the Word became flesh and lived among us, so a service-church also takes on the flesh of the world and lives among people of this land. "Glory to God in the highest heaven, and on earth peace among those whom he favours!" (Luke 2:14). This Good News arrives in the world without judgment but establishes a perpetual peace. A service-church is called to exemplify this peace in the disjointed world. Just as God has chosen the lowly shepherds to reveal the forthcoming jubilation, a service-church will be in solidarity with the lowly to celebrate hope. As Athanasius once observed: God has become a human person, so that we may share God's divinity.

Service-church is the Body of Christ. Within the invisible Christ, the physical body of the church includes every person within the duty of pastoral care, and an agency involves all staff serving the corporate interest. The Body of Christ invites the church and the service into mutual dialogue and life-giving exchange through the unity of the Spirit in the bonds of peace (Eph 4:3). Indeed, the body does not consist of one member but of many (1 Cor 12:14). Paul reminds the early church of a simple truth. One part of the body cannot say to the other that "I have no need of you." Instead, to be one body means clothing the less honourable with greater honour and treating the less respectable with greater respect. For Paul, this principle of uplifting the weak indicates how God's creation orders also the human body. The body has its own priority to support its weakest part so that life can be prolonged.

Ancient Daoism has a political philosophy developed from medical practice. It is called "Preserving Qi and Loving People 养气爱民." Governing a nation is like preserving health. Having scripts to treat diseases is an inferior method when compared to mastering the art of longevity. Preventive medicine aims to cultivate the embodied living force of Qi within the bodily "Cinnabar Fields." A strong body becomes the best defence against all diseases. Likewise, governing a country is to love the people. People are the collective Qi of the society, and so loving people becomes the primary method to enhance the health of a civilisation. The longevity of a person and prolongation of a dynasty are akin. The essence of politics is not the will to power but the preservation of life.

Service-church preserves life within the Body of Christ. Instead of looking to an otherworldly salvation of the soul, it anticipates the kingdom of God breaking into the present. Its mission is driven not by the evangelical proclamation of the Word but by following God's incarnation through personal care, community building, and the advocacy of a just society. This shifts the ground of theological conversation, from one of moral teaching to the discovery of God's Spirit at work. Within the circle of theological reflection, faith and deeds are not presumed to be antithetical. By recognising them as both important in the Body of Christ, it shifts our perspective from text to context, from tradition to experience, and views the latter as equally valid paths to further understand God.

The UCA at its formation rightly recognised the church as the fellowship of the Spirit, the beginning of a new creation. "The Church as the fellowship of the Holy Spirit confesses Jesus as the Lord over its own life; it also confesses that Jesus is Head over all things, the beginning of a new creation, of a new humanity" (BoU, §3). The church as a whole receives its members through baptism and celebrates the fellowship of Christ through holy Communion. But ecclesial identity does not stop at the sacraments. Faith communities by nature are the beginning of a new creation with the potency of the Spirit of resurrection. They extend the fellowship of the Spirit into the world as the beginning of a new humanity. Community services work on the other side of this fellowship by building new communities. They are, as such, fundamentally part of the

UCA, reminding all citizens of that unifying vision whose end is an inclusive and reconciled world.

The Assembly Standing Committee received a recent report from the Australian Regional and Remote Community Services (ARRCS). The report reflects a three-year transition that UnitingCare agencies undertook over aged care and related services previously run by Frontier Services. Back in 2013, the Department of Health and Ageing enforced sanctions upon the Assembly following serious concerns about the quality of aged care services. As a result, the Assembly faced large financial and ongoing viability challenges. The "Approved Provider" status of Assembly was at risk, and the reputation of the church as a reliable community service provider was in doubt. The crisis really tested the relationship between the church and the service. To take on the management of these services meant instituting a process for resolving a range of financial, property, and regulatory matters. Every one of these required a high level of professional skills and financial contribution from the network. "It's hard. But it is the church. How could we not do it?" commented Colleen Gayer.

We are the Body of Christ. "If one member suffers, all suffer together with it; if one member is honoured, all rejoice together with it" (1 Cor 12:26). It was through a moment of crisis that the whole issue of mission came into focus—serving the Indigenous people. The commitment of UCA service promotion in remote Australia had to remain secure. The transition would not have happened without the collaboration of the Assembly and Queensland Synod with the strong support from UnitingCare network, particularly Blue Care and Juniper. Now the ARRCS has enhanced the quality of care and achieved an overall surplus within the three-year transition. The spirit of collaboration led to the further development of partnerships helping sustain its operation in remote communities. Training Indigenous staff has become a core value in the operation, this includes community building as the long-term solution to community problems.[23]

Theologically speaking, this is a story of death and resurrection. Christ "calls people into the fellowship of his suffering, to be the disciples of a crucified Lord; in his own strange way Christ constitutes, rules and renews them as his Church" (BoU, §4). The crisis prompted three lessons:

- The church was out of its depth in the highly regulated services environment funded by government, and professional skills were required to meet compliance standards.
- The church can no longer live in an enclosed circle of accountability. The model of cooperation, involving the government, the church, the agency, and the communities, has enabled the mission to continue and to grow in the remote communities.
- UnitingCare network provided the human, professional, and financial resources required to make the transition possible. They enhanced the UCA capacity to participate in the challenging environment of God's mission today.

The term "crisis" in Chinese is made of two characters: danger and opportunity, 危机.

This crisis is Christ's strange way to make his body bigger and stronger. As the head of the body, he calls people into his suffering with the Indigenous people and draws human resources from all walks of life into the covenanting relationship of the UCA with the First Peoples. For the

---

[23] The information was provided by Heather Waterson in her report to the Assembly Standing Committee, March 2016.

Assembly, the transition was costly and painful, but nothing was lost in the grace of God. While the transition was stressful for the UnitingCare network, the crisis enabled the growth of its capacity through collaboration. Our uniting journey is still in the making. The Body of Christ will continue to be shaped by the fellowship of the Spirit; we grow through building internal and external relationships.

Instead of looking at the ARRCS as service to the First Peoples, there is an even bigger lesson to be learnt here. The whole church is learning about its whole mission, in and through service, with those who are "at the margins." They are, in fact, helping the church discover afresh its own mission and identity. This lesson presses home the whole discussion of the unity of mission and purpose of being service-church.

Conclusion

The Daoist philosopher Zhuangzi (370–287 BCE), a contemporary of Aristotle, once wrote about the Butterfly Dream. One night he dreamed that he was a butterfly. In the dream he was happy; the butterfly was overlooking his village and moving over rivers to a distant land. When he woke up, he did not really know whether he was a man who had just awoken or whether he was actually the butterfly. He never answered this question. But he presented to us an existential question that we could not escape. Are we just dreaming about happiness and see the free butterfly as our true destiny? Or is the butterfly actually dreaming to be a human being?

The moral is that we will always live in this tension. The church and the service are not two distinct identities of the UCA. It is up to us to see through the difference, so that we can live as one life.

The Word became flesh and lived among the people. This ancient tale of "God with us" tells us that God not only dreams but becomes a person. The incarnation invites the whole UCA to mirror "God with us." It is, among other things, a call for the UCA to take on the flesh of ancient cultures and live among the First Peoples. This unfolding life of "God with us" will make us increasingly multicultural and far more colourful. It will draw all people, stakeholders, resources into the common purpose of preserving life.

This creation of the Spirit will weave us together into an interconnected life. At the heart of this life is reconciliation. In a post-Christian society, it is indeed a real challenge to witness to Christ in government-funded community services in Australia. It is a constant reminder that "God with us" is God's witness to the world.[24] The collaboration of the church and the service will keep the Body of Christ open and allow God to reconcile the world to God's self in Christ Jesus.

It is true that Zhuangzi never answered his own question of the Butterfly Dream. However, when we have freed ourselves from the weight of our own assumptions—the quest for personal salvation—we are able to fly as the butterfly. Then we would realise that we are not on our own but are caught in the unfolding Spirit of God's partaking in our lives. Our answer to Zhuangzi's existential question would actually be to dissolve the difference between the two worlds.

---

[24] John G. Flett, *The Witness of God: The Trinity, missio Dei, Karl Barth, and the Nature of Christian Community* (Grand Rapids, MI: Eerdmans, 2010).

Communicating the Gospel in Plural Places: Theology, Church Theory, and the Sociological Aspects of Contemporary Church Practice

Annette Noller

For the past thirty years, practical theology in Germany has worked with theories of the church built on sociological interpretations of what is occurring within the church. Collected from members and non-members, these surveys have revealed a good deal of important data concerning the perceived relationship of church and diaconia in terms of its meaning, the variety of its personal engagements, and the importance of church affiliation.[1] Sociological theories, such as system theory, inspired practical theology to think about church and diaconia in innovative ways. One of the insights recognizes that churches develop in modern and differentiated societies not only in one social form but in a plurality of organizational

---

[1] See Evangelische Kirche in Deutschland, ed., *Engagement und Indifferenz: Kirchenmitgliedschaft als soziale Praxis: V. EKD-Erhebung über Kirchenmitgliedschaft* (Hannover: EKD, 2014); Heinrich Bedford-Strohm and Volker Jung, eds., *Vernetzte Vielfalt: Kirche angesichts von Individualisierung und Säkularisierung; Die fünfte Erhebung über Kirchenmitgliedschaft* (Gütersloh: Gütersloher Verlagshaus, 2015; Jan Hermelink, *Praktische Theologie der Kirchenmitgliedschaft: Interdisziplinäre Untersuchungen zur Gestaltung kirchlicher Beteiligung* (Göttingen: Vandenhoeck & Ruprecht, 2000).

forms.[2] As part of the church's mission, it is called to communicate the gospel to all peoples (Mark 16:15; Matt 28:18-20). The very difference of these people means also that the church should not rely on only one shape of organization but should seek a plurality of forms.

Some results from a larger German research project will be discussed in this chapter. Based on theological and sociological insights, it shows how both parishes *and* diaconal agencies develop church in different forms and engagements. This follows a line of thinking that the church develops as a so called "hybrid"[3] organization in plural places.[4]

Church Theory: Theological and Sociological Descriptions of the Church

Since 1972, the Evangelische Kirche in Deutschland (EKD) has commissioned representative surveys regarding church membership. These surveys were based on sociological methods and via the use of questionnaires and interviews. Members

---

[2] See Annette Noller, *Diakonat und Kirchenreform. Empirische, historische und ekklesiologische Dimensionen einer diakonischen Kirche* (Stuttgart: Kohlhammer, 2016); Annette Noller, "Diakonat und Kirchenreform: Beiträge der Diakonatsforschung zur Kirchentheorie und -praxis," *Praktische Theologie* 51, no. 4 (2016): 234–41.

[3] Eberhard Hauschildt, "Hybrid evangelische Großkirche vor einem Schub an Organisationswerdung: Anmerkungen zum Impulspapier 'Kirche der Freiheit' des Rates der EKD und zur Zukunft der Evangelischen Kirche zwischen Kongregationalisierung, Filialisierung und Regionalisierung," *Pastoraltheologie* 96, no. 1 (2007): 56–66, here 56.

[4] See Noller, *Diakonat und Kirchenreform*; Uta Pohl-Patalong, *Von der Ortskirche zu kirchlichen Orten: Ein Zukunftsmodell*, 2nd ed. (Göttingen: Vandenhoeck & Ruprecht, 2006); Uta Pohl-Patalong and Eberhard Hauschildt, eds., *Kirche verstehen* (Gütersloh: Gütersloher Verlagshaus, 2016).

along with non-members were questioned every ten years concerning their relation to, engagement with, and expectations of belonging to the church. These investigations were accompanied by broader sociological research, including investigation into different milieus, social system theories (Niklas Luhmann), social and missionary parish development, conversion and re-entry into the church.

As an example of the results, a 2013 survey found that about 60 percent of all inhabitants in Germany are Christians. The two biggest churches are the state Protestant and Roman Catholic churches. Each hold about 30 percent of membership. There continues to be decline in membership, especially in former socialist areas, but the basic alliance to the church seems to have remained consistent for the past forty years. While some do not feel very close to the church in terms of belief, most members retain their commitment to the institution. Though a great number have retained their church membership, only 10 to 15 percent of all members participate in local parishes and in church services. Yet, the latest survey, one that draws on the baseline data of 2012, found that 73 percent of the questioned members "categorically" exclude the possibility of leaving their church.[5] This figure corresponds to a similar pattern found in each of the four past surveys. It indicates that people are bonded to the church not only through individual engagement with a local parish. Although pastors and parishes are the best known and most representative public persons and institutions in churches, other criteria for belonging and remaining in the church exist.[6]

---

[5] See "Einleitung," in *Engagement und Indifferenz*, 17.
[6] Other recurrent data over the last five surveys bear out this conclusion; see Noller, *Diakonat und Kirchenreform*, esp. 49–73.

Central here are the expectations people have regarding the church and diaconal engagement. A 2012 survey (published in 2015) asked a question concerning where and how the church should engage itself.[7] Eighty-three percent of those questioned, members and non-members, indicated that as first and second priorities areas concerning the church's social engagement. This included the statement that the "church should help people in need." Worship services and prayer followed only as the third and fourth priorities. This result replicates the importance attributed to diaconal work in each of the previous surveys: members and non-members expect the church to engage in diaconal service even when they themselves have no immediate need of it.

As to how we might interpret this data, Arnold Gehlen developed a social theory dealing with the fulfillment of needs against the backdrop of everyday life.[8] According to Gehlen, the development from archaic civilization to modern culture required institutions in the background that afforded a sense of security. Humankind needs institutions that are reliable in meeting needs that they alone are not able to provide. According to this theory, most members of the church expect that the church as an institution will work helpfully against the multitude of dangers and distresses in daily life. People need this awareness of support when life and family are endangered by social or health risks. Furthermore, following Niklas Luhmann, these institutions help give some sense

---

[7] Gerhard Wegner and Anja Schädel, "Diakonische Potenziale," in *Engagement und Indifferenz*, 93–95, here 93 (image 1); Noller, *Diakonat und Kirchenreform*, 69–71.

[8] Arnold Gehlen, *Urmensch und Spätkultur: Philosophische Ergebnisse und Aussagen* (Bonn: Athenäum Verlag, 1956), 50–54, here 50; Noller, *Diakonat und Kirchenreform*, 439–42.

to the contingency of life.⁹ We expect these institutions to communicate hope and comfort in times of distress and disaster. Due to its long tradition of diaconal engagement, churches in Germany are perceived to be institutions that provide help and support in the social background.

Social engagement is one of the main tasks of church activities. The activities of church agencies are an expression of Christian belief and so are central to the church's mission. Charity and advocacy deepen the acceptance and reputation of the churches in modern societies. Diaconal engagement is an area where many believers in Germany engage with their faith, both in attitude and action. Public opinion concerning the church's role in society may well have changed within the context of more individual and plural ways of religious life.[10] Some clear criticisms have developed concerning diaconal activity due to the dominance of public financing and the influence of a market economy. These factors notwithstanding, however, the diaconal activities of associations, agencies, and churches have good reputations and remain high in public esteem. Church members remain church members not only because of prayers and sermons but also because of the church's social responsibilities. Church taxes and donations are also personal contributions to faith and charity.

To return to the surveys conducted by the EKD, a further finding was that members were connected to the church in

---

[9] Niklas Luhmann, *Soziale Systeme: Grundriß einer allgemeinen Theorie* (Frankfurt a.M.: Suhrkamp, 1984), 92–107.

[10] *Engagement und Indifferenz*, 108–16; Johannes Eurich and Wolfgang Maaser, *Diakonie in der Sozialökonomie: Studien zu Folgen der neuen Wohlfahrtspolitik* (Leipzig: Evangelische Verlagsanstalt, 2013).

so-called distanced ways.[11] Not all people want to join parishes consistently and continuously. Most members structure their relation to the church through temporary contacts. Most members maintain contact with the church in the rites marking life's passages or biographical turning points as celebrated in occasional services. Baptism for babies, confirmation for the youth, weddings, and burials—all are still viewed as important spiritual and celebratory events for families and individuals. Occasional contact, such as Christmas and Easter services, are also important given the significance of their meaning for the faith through the church year. These celebrations, often experienced as highlights in daily life, are important spiritual resources for believers. In these occasional and church year services, the church accompanies believers by interrupting their daily lives and creating spaces for sacred festivity in the presence of God.[12]

Occasional contact with the church reinforces the importance of religious socialization and education. Theories about religious socialization show that for believers in the Christian God, the most important education takes place in childhood within families, in kindergartens, and in schools. Confirmation classes as well as adult education offered by the church help to deepen belief. Peter Bubmann and other theorists of religious education have observed the importance of non-regular opportunities such as conferences, retreats, and the famous German "Kirchentage," which are visited by believers like a

---

[11] EKD, ed., *Engagement und Indifferenz*, 9. See Noller, *Diakonat und Kirchenreform*, 61–71.

[12] See Noller, *Diakonat und Kirchenreform*, 75–80. On the significance of "causal praxis," see Michael Meyer-Blank and Birgit Weyel, *Studien- und Arbeitsbuch Praktische Theologie* (Göttingen: UTB, 2008), 83–93.

"spiritual oasis" on their way through everyday life.[13] Contact with the churches occurs, in other words, in educational areas such as religious instruction in public schools, in the telling of narratives in families and church kindergartens, in religious adult education, and in church media. All these offerings invite participation in occasions of religious communication; all are part of communicating the gospel. Communicating the gospel in this plurality of place is necessary to reach members and non-members within their different individual biographies and milieus. Within German practical theology, this diversity of gospel communication in diverse "modi" is one of the main tasks of churches in socially differentiated modern societies. It challenges us to think about the church acting and developing in plural places—not only in parishes, but also in areas such as those identified with the diaconal, casual, cultural, media, and educational areas.

Uta Pohl-Patalong was the first to observe that, while in history and at present parishes were quite important in the development of the church, the church *never* developed *only* in the shape of congregations.[14] Through church history, the Christian faith spread in plural forms within a wide focus of diaconal and religious education and informational offerings. Eberhard Hauschild named this multi-perspectival phenomenon of churches: "hybrid.[15] Like modern cars, running on petrol and solar power, the church has also to develop on the basis of different sources. Churches need flexible motors

---

[13] Peter Bubmann, "Die Zeit der Gemeinde: Kirchliche Bildungsorte zwischen Kirche auf Dauer und Kirche bei Gelegenheit," in *Gemeindepädagogik*, ed. Peter Bubmann et al. (Berlin: De Gruyter, 2012), 91.

[14] Uta Pohl-Patalong, "Gemeinde in historischer Perspektive," in *Gemeindepädagogik*, 37–60.

[15] See footnote 3

to run effectively. Therefore, church theorists recommend a focus not only on the parochial shape of churches but on plural forms. For Bishop Heinrich Bedford-Strohm, president of the EKD, today the role of church cannot be limited to the local. Its role is properly a social and public one because churches want to be engaged in daily life, in social questions, in religious education, and in public media.[16]

A church developing in plural places should widen its perspective. This means local engagement in parishes, but also engagement in the diaconal and educational, in the cultural and public areas where the gospel is communicated with members and non-members in a modern society.[17]

Diaconal Theology and Diaconal Practice

To summarize the argument to this point, the church is an organization which develops in plural, hybrid forms and places. Diaconal engagement is one of them. Social engagement communicates the gospel in word and in social action. It is a specific way to proclaim the gospel. We turn now to the specific question of the diaconal engagement of the church.[18]

---

[16] Heinrich Bedford-Strohm, "Nachgedacht: Thesen zur öffentlichen Theologie," http://www.bayern-evangelisch.de/www/glauben/gedanken-zum-reformationsfest-von-heinrich-bedford-strohm.php; Heinrich Bedford-Strohm, "Diakonie in der Perspektive 'öffentlicher Theologie'," in *Von der 'Barmherzigkeit' zum 'Sozial-Markt': Zur Ökonomisierung der sozialdiakonischen Dienste*, ed. Heinrich Bedford-Strohm et al. (Gütersloh: Gütersloher Verlagshaus, 2008), 19–32.

[17] See Noller, *Diakonat und Kirchenreform*, 84–86, 428–45.

[18] See Noller, *Diakonat und Kirchenreform*, 23–32; Heinz Schmidt, "Biblische Grundlagen der Diakonie," in *Das Geschenk der Solidarität: Chancen und Herausforder-*

Diaconia and the Gospel

The good news of the gospel is that God's love is revealed in Jesus Christ. The central theme of Christ's incarnation is the message of God's love for God's fallible creation. This love is visible in God's redemption for all sinners. It is visible in the way that God intends to restore community and the creation. In Jesus Christ, God becomes human. God shares God's own life with people in spiritual and social need, in illness and poverty. God provides community to those who are poor spiritually and socially. God is involved with those who are religious and socially stigmatized and marginalized. This diaconal impact of the gospel can be found in the narratives of Jesus Christ. It can be seen at the theological centre of redemption. In Christ's crucifixion and resurrection, the salvation of not only individuals but also the whole of creation is in view. Individual justification is embedded in visions of social justice and peace and the renewal of the whole creation. Christ's messiahship is interpreted in the tradition of liberating and comforting grace. It is told within a critical context in relation to domination and exploitation, especially in the advocacy tradition of the exodus and prophetic traditions. The vision of the kingdom of God promises life in brother-sisterhood and solidarity. That is why the famous German theologian Dietrich Bonhoeffer said that believers have to both pray and practice justice.[19]

---

ungen der Diakonie in Frankreich und Deutschland, ed. Fritz Lienhard and Heinz Schmidt (Heidelberg: Universitätsverlag Winter, 2006), 112–33.

[19] "[O]ur being Christians today will be limited to two things: prayer and righteous action among [people]. All Christian thinking, speaking, and organizing must be born anew out of this prayer and action." Dietrich Bonhoeffer, *Letters and Papers from Prison* (London: SCM, 2001), 105.

Social engagement is at the centre of the gospel. It is not something that can be occasionally added or left over. Charity and advocacy are not a second or third aspect after others, such as preaching and praying. They are central to the gospel which commands us to "love God and love your neighbour as yourself" (Luke 10:27). Practicing charity and diaconal service is a form of the imitation of Christ. The liturgies of early Christianity connected eucharistic communion to the care for the ill and for poor members. Deacons were advised by their bishops to bring donations from agape meals to those unable to attend. Deacons were ordered to look after those who suffered, the ill and poor members of congregations. Nor was this charity limited to members—it was also for needy neighbours in pagan surroundings. With this selfless attitude, charity supported the mission and the growth of the church. Charity pervaded the church's history. It was practiced in the monastic tradition and, at the time of the Reformation, considered the responsibility of all believers, no matter their occupation or social status. In nineteenth-century Germany, diaconal foundations were maintained during the industrial revolution. Theologians like Johann Heinrich Wichern built so-called rescue homes to educate and support children from socially disadvantaged families, and educated deacons to rescue starving and underprivileged children from physical and spiritual distress. Believers like Theodor Fliedner founded diaconal "mother houses" and educated deaconesses to support the poor and nurture especially the ill among them.[20]

---

[20] On the history of the diaconate, see Noller, *Diakonat und Kirchenreform*, 209–366; Annette Noller, "Der Diakonat – historische Entwicklungen und gegenwärtige Herausforderungen," in *Diakonat – theologische und sozialwissenschaftliche Perspektiven auf ein kirchliches Amt*, eds. Annette Noller, Ellen Eidt, and Heinz Schmidt (Stuttgart: Kohlhammer, 2013), 42–84.

These nineteenth-century foundations still exist in Germany. They were founded as tax-free associations and organised alongside the church as religious institutions. Today the Catholic *Caritas* and the Protestant *Diakonie* are the two biggest social associations in Germany. Together, they employ about one million people (each at about five hundred thousand) and have an equal number of volunteers. In a subsidiary cooperation with state actors and municipal providers, they operate within the German welfare state.[21] The main financial support comes through taxes, payouts from insurance companies, other public resources, and private donations. There is also a large international diaconal service through German agencies such as Brot für die Welt (Bread for the World). Beside these large and powerful agencies, there continue to be charity activities through congregations and church districts, financed in the main by church taxes and sponsorship.

In the last years, some critical discussions have arisen concerning whether and to what extent these big associations are able to act within the tradition of Christian faith. This question emerges when employees of big diaconal enterprises of about a thousand employees no longer hold to the Christian faith. Moreover, it is not the churches but the system of social welfare legislation which controls and regulates the content of their work. In German diaconal work, the ground of such activity in the faith is often invisible to cooperation partners and clients. A lack of adequate funding and the ongoing struggle for resources in a so-called social market economy has strengthened this discussion of the Christian profile of actual diaconal work.

---

[21] See Ulli Arnold, Klaus Grunwald, Bernd Maelicke, eds., *Lehrbuch Sozialwirtschaft*, 4th ed. (Baden-Baden: Nomos, 2014).

Diaconal Profile: Diaconal Corporate Culture and Mission Statements

Is it possible to promote diaconal engagement as a special form of church if clients and cooperation partners no longer recognize any Christian form and meaning? In what way might diaconal engagement be visible as a form of Christian belief? In answer to these questions, researchers in Germany have suggested the formation of a diaconal "proprium" or a so-called Protestant profile.

One proposal focuses on developing a diaconal profile by elaborating on a diaconal corporate culture. Today, analysts of global concerns as well as diaconal theorists examine the "soft factors" of an enterprise. Soft factors include mission statements, behaviours, attitudes, shared ethics, corporate design, and the working atmosphere. Culture in this context means all instruments and factors that form the specific appearance and atmosphere of an organization. This culture is shared consciously or unconsciously by the staff of a diaconal enterprise. Some aspects of the enterprise's culture are visible and developed in statements that reflect their traditions and ordered structure. Yet, as Beate Hofmann has demonstrated, a culture's main roots usually remain invisible, belonging to the inarticulate traditions and habits of the staff and the leaders of an organization.[22] These traditional values can be reinforced by management strategies, such as through a culture of remembrance for institutional founders, and in celebratory events which include spiritual offerings in the form of prayers and devotions. Diaconal culture can be strengthened through developing a humane working atmosphere that provides

---

[22] See Beate Hofmann, *Diakonische Unternehmenskultur* (Stuttgart: Kohlhammer, 2008); Cornelia Coenen-Marx, *Die Seele des Sozialen: Diakonische Energien für den sozialen Zusammenhalt* (Neukirchen-Vluyn: Neukirchener Verlag, 2013).

possibilities for interaction and the expression of complaints. It can be formed by team discussions about ethics or in counselling sessions.

A common instrument for developing diaconal culture in Germany is the production of a mission statement. In these statements, diaconal providers formulate their main values and strategic aims in key sentences. These sentences usually grow out of an integrative process between the leaders and staff of a diaconal enterprise or agency. It involves the entire staff in a process of thinking about the main values and visions of their work. The process assures professionals and volunteers of the aims and values in their working environment. The mission statement summarises the culture and values of a diaconal enterprise and this is made available in such public platforms as the institution's website. Clients and cooperative partners can access information about the organizational identity and operative aims of a diaconal provider.

To develop a diaconal culture in this way, staff members and leaders need to have open discussions concerning their diaconal ethics, attitudes, and traditions. One of the most important options in developing diaconal culture, the habits and actions in agencies, lies in the further education of employees, staff, and leaders so as to deepen their ethical and theological knowledge.

Diaconal Education, Diaconal Professionals, and Ministries

Fostering plural ways of communicating the gospel in congregations as well as in diaconal agencies requires volunteers and professionals educated in diaconal practice. Many German agencies provide professional development for their employees.

One component of this professional development focuses on Christian beliefs, diaconal traditions, and ethics. Most employees in German diaconal agencies are members of Christian churches. An increasing number are not. Basic knowledge of the Christian gospel, the confessions, and diaconal traditions is decreasing. Further education, conferences, and lectures are important instruments that bring colleagues into discourse with Protestant attitudes, ethics, and belief.

Alongside these options, Germany has a long and profound tradition of diaconal professionals known as deaconesses and deacons (Christian social workers and nurses). These professional traditions, which were founded in the nineteenth century by Johann Hinrich Wichern, Theodor Fliedner, and their colleagues, still exist in Protestant German churches. These (male and female) deacons are predominantly in health and nursing care as well as in social work. The Protestant tradition views them as supportive church professionals who proclaim the gospel in God's mission, not so much through the Word as through social engagement. These diaconal professionals obtain a "dual professional qualification." Sixty-two percent attain a double bachelor's in deaconry and social work, and the others combine deaconry with nursing and early childhood education. These various social professions can be combined with a qualification in theological and diaconal competences, where they learn pastoral counselling, preaching, ethics, and theology.[23] With such a grounding in the Christian tradition, these social service professionals help influence the culture of social agencies and diaconal enterprises.[24]

In my local church in southern Germany (Evangelische Landeskirche in Württemberg), we had a project in which a team of professors from Ludwigsburg and Heidelberg evaluated the work of deacons.[25] As one example, one deaconess was responsible for counselling families where a parent had died. As a professional social worker, she organized the needed assistance as allowed by the state, including financial support for the widowed parent and school or nursing care for the children. But as a deacon of the church, she provided spiritual care by communicating hope and comfort based on religious belief. This is possible even in interreligious settings. In our evaluation discussions, she described her work as giving professional practical help along with the essential component of supporting widows and children. This allowed some measure of hope and encouraged the conviction that in the distress and disorder of extreme situations of mourning there will be a future in which to maintain and reorganize life.[26]

---

[23] Graduates from these study programs can be ordained as deacons in some German churches. A 2012 survey found that there were fifty-six diaconal and community-pedagogy study programs in Germany, educating more than 1,200 graduates each year. In 2013, the umbrella organization for all Protestant deacons included about 19,000 members. See Annette Noller and Peter Höfflin, *Diakonische und gemeindepädagogische Studien- und Ausbildungsgänge: Eine Erhebung im Raum der EKD* (Stuttgart: Verlag der Evangelischen Gesellschaft, 2015)

[24] Noller, *Diakonat und Kirchenreform*, 99–132.

[25] Werner Baur et al., eds., *Diakonat für die Kirche der Zukunft* (Stuttgart: Kohlhamer, 2016).

[26] Bauer, *Diakonat*, 71–80.

In evaluating fifteen different projects, we discovered the wide spread of diaconal work in communities and society in general.[27] In every project, the church was seen to be present and close to people's daily needs through the work done by deacons. Each project embodied the gospel in different ways: in social and spiritual counselling or in different services that occurred apart from the weekly Sunday services in parishes. Small services were done with volunteers in diaconal shops, with children in schools, with self-help groups for widows and their children, with prayers and meditations in youth excursions, in diaconal nursing stations, and in other plural situations and forms. It was clear that this type of diaconal communication of the gospel does not use the same formal theological language as found in a parish service. In its liturgies and sermons, this service was oriented to everyday language and situations.

Often the church background of the deacons was invisible. They were seen primarily as social workers. Nevertheless, there was awareness, shared by their cooperation partners and clients, that they were "somehow connected with church." While their communication of the gospel was embedded in social or nursing action, it was, nonetheless, a special type of gospel in action and a part of the church's communication. In every case, clients and cooperating partners recognized deacons as sent by their church through their attitudes,

---

[27] See Noller, *Diakonat und Kirchenreform,* 132–208.

their ethics, their counselling and comforting, and their communicating and serving the gospel.[28]

Diaconal service has long encountered this range of opportunities to communicate the gospel through all of society. In the nineteenth century, Jochen Christoph Kaiser pointed out that deacons and deaconesses communicated belief using everyday language and within the milieu that they shared with their clients. For Kaiser, mother and brotherhood diaconia developed precisely along this religiously differentiated performance and reached thereby a high missionary range.[29] It might be promising to consider a specific Christian education for social workers, nurses, and community educators that enables them as social, nursing, and pedagogical professionals to communicate Christian ethics and attitudes in their workplaces. They could preach and pray in their working area if possible, contingent on the nature of the institution.

In both the tradition and in current practice, diaconal approaches provide more possibilities for close contact with everyday life and problems. Social engagement can lead to ethical conflicts and controversies caused by the intervention of social legislation and competitive market economies. In these fractured and controversial forms of action, the diaconal providers, who are governed by state legislation, can still

---

[28] See Annette Noller, "Diakonat und Seelsorge: Zur Rekonstruktion seelsorgerlichen Handelns von Diakoninnen und Diakonen," in *Evaluation im Diakonat: Sozialwissenschaftliche Vermessung diakonischer Praxis*, ed. Ellen Eidt and Claudia Schulz (Stuttgart: Kohlhammer, 2013), 376–405; Annette Noller, "Diakonat und theologische Kompetenz," in *Evaluation im Diakonat*, 406–31.

[29] Jochen-Christoph Kaiser, "Sozialer Protestantismus als 'kirchliche Zweitstruktur' [2001]," in *Studienbuch Diakonik, vol. 2: Diakonisches Handeln, diakonisches Profil, diakonische Kirche*, ed. Volker Herrmann and Martin Horstmann (Neukirchen-Vluyn: Neukirchener Verlag, 2006), 259–79, esp. 278; Noller, *Diakonat und Kirchenreform*, 437–39.

be criticized by other believers. The gospel continues to communicate, however, within the fallibility of creation through active advocacy in the political areas of society. To give up diaconal engagement in its various forms, in agencies and enterprises, could mean giving up a form of communicating the gospel in a wide area of society and daily life and giving up responsibilities for social and health needs.

It might be promising to think about plural forms of Christian education for different professions and ministries to enable colleagues in diaconal agencies to deal with ethical dilemmas and challenges in awareness of a Christian tradition. Having multi-professional teams of Christian social workers, diaconal nurses, theologians, pastors, religious community educators, and parish workers will help develop a church that can communicate the gospel in plural places.

Conclusion

Communicating the gospel is the main purpose of churches. This communication happens in differentiated societies in plural places. While the gospel has to be proclaimed in parishes mainly by pastors, it can also be communicated in plural places in the form of education and diaconal action by various ministries, professions, and volunteers. It has to be communicated through social and public media.[30]

At the centre of all strategies for a church that is spread over plural places, such as congregations, communities, and society, is reference to God's redeeming grace and the mission

---

[30] On the communication of the gospel as the central task of the church, see Christian Grethlein, *Praktische Theologie* (Berlin: De Gruyter, 2012); Noller, *Diakonat und Kirchenreform*, 92–95, 442–45.

to preach hope to the suffering creation (Rom 8:18-25). This can be done through worship, preaching, receiving sacraments—as well as in diaconal service. The Apostle Paul affirmed that Christ's Body has many different parts (1 Cor 12:12ff.; Rom 12:3ff.). The church as the Body of Christ needs eyes, ears, mouths, hands, feet, brain, head, and so on. All limbs, even those that are despised and marginalized, are important for the functioning of Christ's Body. "We cover with honour those limbs which seem to be less valued" (1 Cor 12:23). Paul's ecclesiology looks to the participation of every diverse charism and talent. It is an inclusive concept, for "if one limb is suffering all limbs are suffering" (1 Cor 12:26). This embodiment of Christ happens in the whole creation. It unfolds in a church that acts and communicates in plural places, in diverse forms and milieus, and thereby in differentiated social systems as a religious and socially responsible actor in modern society.

Does Theology Matter? Or How Church-Related Agencies Can Become (or Not) an Extension of the State

Douglas Hynd

Introduction

A number of factors inform the current shape of church-related social welfare agencies[1] in Australia: historical influences from the United Kingdom, geography, a pragmatically pluralist constitutional settlement, and a continuously shifting engagement with government. One of the more significant influences in the 1990s was the move by governments to contract for the provision of social welfare and human services. I have written elsewhere on research into the impact of this shift, focusing especially on how it led some agencies to lose touch with their founding identity and mission and become an extension of the state. The research covered agencies from a broad spectrum of denominations, providing a good basis for comparing differing ecclesiological and governance arrangements and

---

[1] On the rationale for the use of the terminology of "church-related agencies," see Doug Hynd, "What's in a Name? Social Welfare Agencies Engagement with Government Beyond 'Religious', 'Faith-Based' and 'Secular' Terminology," *Third Sector Review* 20, no. 1 (2014): 163–83.

identifying the presence or absence of theology in shaping agency responses to contracting.[2]

In this article, I reflect on the role played by theology in influencing and accounting for the consequences of contracting engagement by agencies with the state. My account begins with the circumstances which led agencies to participate in contracting. I then explore the way theology was present or absent in the rationales offered for agency participation, particularly the experience of the Salvation Army in contracting to provide offshore humanitarian services for asylum seekers and Catholic agencies involved in contracting for the provision of employment services. Theology emerges as a significant factor in decision making about contracting in the second of these narratives, but not the first. Theological commitments also appear to be relevant to the shaping of some of the tactics used by agencies to maintain their identity and mission.[3]

---

[2] Douglas Hynd, "On (Not) 'Becoming an Extension of the State' while 'Seeking the Flourishing of the City': A Theologically-Informed Inquiry into the Impact on 'Church-Related' Agencies of Contracting with Government to Provide Social Welfare and Human Services in Australia, 1996–2013" (PhD diss., Australian Catholic University, 2017).

[3] On theological and philosophical issues with regard to church-related agencies, see Rana Jawad, *Religion and Faith-Based Welfare: From Wellbeing to Ways of Being* (Bristol: Policy Press, 2012); Luke Bretherton, *Christianity & Contemporary Politics: The Conditions and Possibilities of Faithful Witness* (Oxford: Wiley-Blackwell, 2010); Paul Cloke, Samuel Thomas, and Andrew Williams, "Radical Faith Praxis? Exploring the Changing Theological Landscape of Christian Faith Motivation," in *Faith-Based Organisations and Exclusion in European Cities*, ed. Justin Beaumont and Paul Cloke (Bristol: Policy Press, 2012).

Findings of the Inquiry

I framed the inquiry theologically with reference to a trajectory of ongoing tension. This tension consists of seeking the flourishing of the city, on the one hand, while maintaining an exilic identity, on the other,[4] a tension which was at risk of collapse in church-related social welfare agencies in the context of their contracting with government.[5] While drawing on interviews with senior management in agencies, I also undertook documentary analysis of agency annual reports and website publications to test sociological accounts about the likely impacts of contracting in identifying tactics of agency resistance and response.

Alasdair McIntyre observes that the nation-state "is a dangerous and unmanageable institution, presenting itself on the one hand as a bureaucratic supplier of goods and services, which is always about to, but never actually does, give its clients value for money, and on the other as a repository of sacred values, which from time to time invites one to lay down

---

[4] On the term "flourishing," see Nicholas Wolterstorff, *Until Justice and Peace Embrace: The Kuyper Lectures for 1981* (Grand Rapids, MI: Eerdmans, 1983), 69–72; "Justice and Peace," in *New Dictionary of Christian Ethics and Pastoral Theology*, ed. David J. Atkinson and David H. Field (Leicester: Inter-Varsity Press, 1995), 19–21. More generally on this tension, see Walter Brueggemann, *Cadences of Home: Preaching among Exiles* (Louisville, KY: Westminster John Knox Press, 1997). On the background to the letter, see Daniel L. Smith, "Jeremiah as Prophet of Nonviolent Resistance," *Journal for the Study of the Old Testament* 43 (1989): 95–107; Daniel L. Smith-Christopher, *A Biblical Theology of Exile* (Minneapolis, MN: Augsburg Fortress, 2002).

[5] On the literature on organisational sociology, see chapter 5 in Douglas Hynd, "On (Not) 'Becoming an Extension of the State' While 'Seeking the Flourishing of the City'."

one's life on its behalf."⁶ McIntyre here names the nation-state in its dual character as both bureaucratic, that is, secular in Weberian terms, and sacral, the latter manifesting itself through nationalism.⁷

Using this distinction as an interpretive framework assists in understanding how agencies can end up as an extension of the state in two quite different modes of operation. Where the state operated in a bureaucratic mode in contracting for employment services, this involved an increasingly tight specification of outcomes, processes, reporting requirements, and financial incentives to ensure rigid agency compliance with government policy. This form of operation prevented agencies from embodying mission commitments to serve the most vulnerable and facilitate their participation in the wider community.

Also operating in the bureaucratic mode, government contracting in other policy areas stimulated mission drift in agencies through bringing about the importation of a managerialist culture, the demands of which drew management

---

⁶ Alasdair MacIntyre, "A Partial Response to My Critics," in *After MacIntyre: Critical Perspectives on the Work of Alasdair MacIntyre*, ed. John Horton and Susan Mendus (Notre Dame, IN: University of Notre Dame Press, 1994), 303.

⁷ On the character of the state, see Charles Tilly, *Coercion, Capital and European States, AD 990–1992* (Oxford: Blackwell, 1992). The role played by war is emphasised in Charles Tilly, "War Making and State Making as Organized Crime," in *Bringing the State Back In*, ed. Peter Evans, Dietrich Rueschemeyer, and Theda Skocpol (Cambridge: Cambridge University Press, 1985). On the wars of religion and the rise of the nation-state, see William T. Cavanaugh, "'A Fire Strong Enough to Consume the House': The Wars of Religion and the Rise of the State," *Modern Theology* 11, no. 4 (1995): 397–420; William T. Cavanaugh, *The Myth of Religious Violence: Secular Ideology and the Roots of Modern Conflict* (London: Oxford University Press, 2009).

attention away from the agency's mission and purpose. The power imbalance between government and agency resulted in contract provisions that enabled the government to cancel contracts arbitrarily at short notice, to delay decision making about contract renewal, to set payments for services at levels below the cost of their provision, and to index funding provisions to levels that were below the increasing cost of services measured year on year. Contrary to theoretical speculation, there was no evidence to suggest a necessary causal correlation between a high dependence on government funding and a decreased ecclesial connection. Contracting presented, nevertheless, a continuing challenge to agencies' ability to maintain their focus on mission and identity.

Contracting can result in agencies becoming extensions of the state when it is operating in the sacral mode identified by McIntyre. This mode emerged in the operation of the Australian government's policy on refugees and asylum seekers. Here an assertion of state sovereignty in defence of national security came into fundamental conflict with the humanitarian logic of mission commitments of the Salvation Army.

The Significance of Governance

Whether governance arrangements were effective in providing support for agency tactics of resistance to the pressures of contracting critically depended on agency and stakeholder leadership and attention. Catholic diocesan agencies had a clear theological and governance structure within which questions of mission could be, and frequently seem to have been, tested. Exactly how well this ecclesial arrangement worked in maintaining missional identity depended on the leadership of the agency CEO, the interest and support of the bishop, and their mutual relationship in sharing the agency vision with the staff. In the Anglican context, the governance structure of the Brotherhood of St Laurence, predating the contracting era, proved relatively effective in maintaining a reflective process around questions of mission within the agency. Among the other Anglican diocesan agencies, intentional action by leadership in carrying the story of the agency and communicating that to staff were important in either maintaining or loosening that alignment.

Differences in the Uniting Church of Australia governance structure between the various synods offered opportunities for either buffering or amplifying isomorphic pressures arising from contracting.[8] Beyond the major denominational families, maintenance of strong ecclesial identity did not necessarily require an ongoing connection to a denomination or congregation. It did, however, require intentionality in the construction of appropriate governance arrangements and their implementation over time by both the board and CEO to maintain the connection to the Christian movement in its various traditions.

Some agencies actively, and intentionally, responded to the pressures exerted by the bureaucratic character of the state through theological commitments to an account of the person and community not encompassed in the utilitarian calculations and language of policy that shaped government

---

[8] On the risks to Uniting Church agencies, see John Bottomley and Howard N. Wallace, "Risk Management in the New Heaven and the New Earth: Isaiah and *UnitingCare* Victoria and Tasmania's Corporate Governance Policy," *Uniting Church Studies* 13, no. 2 (2007): 1–13; John Bottomley, *In, but Not of the World: A Report on Issues to Strengthen the Faith and Vocation of UnitingCare Chief Executive Officers, Boards and Agencies* (Melbourne, VIC: Creative Ministries Network, 2008).

contracts. Intentional leadership was critical in enabling agencies to resist becoming an extension of the state and was a precondition for effective implementation of tactics of response and resistance. Resistance to the pressures of contracting was not exclusively associated with any specific theological stance or ecclesiology. The role of boards and leadership in owning, communicating, and interpreting the founding story and/or charism of the agency was crucial. Finally, contracting did not have a strong negative impact on agency advocacy. On the contrary, there was an emergent response at a sector level in the development of the denominational coordinating agencies that enabled a coordinated response in policy advocacy.

Agency tactics of response and resistance to the contracting environment included:

- reducing the level of financial dependency on government,
- sustaining partnerships and linkages supportive of mission,
- ensuring active ownership of the founding story or charism by the leadership and board,
- maintaining clarity around governance and alignment with stakeholders in maintaining mission priorities,
- communicating the distinctiveness of agency mission to staff and translating it for staff not familiar with the Christian story.

Theology was an important element in the last three of these tactics.

Theology of the State and Church-Related Agencies Contracting with Government

I previously drew attention to McIntyre's identification of the bureaucratic and the sacral as the two modes of state operation through which agencies could be reduced to being an extension of the state. Let me quickly sketch some underpinnings for this framework as a political and theological orientation.[9]

States are coercion-wielding organisations. A nation-state has, at its core, sovereignty—a singularity of power and authority over life and death, inclusion and exclusion.[10]

---

[9] William Stringfellow, "Jesus Is a Criminal," in *Suspect Tenderness: The Ethics of the Berrigan Witness*, ed. William Stringfellow and Anthony Towne (Eugene, OR: Wipf & Stock, 2005). Terry Eagleton, *Reason, Faith and Revolution: Reflections on the God Debate* (New Haven, CT: Yale University Press, 2009). On the tension between Christianity and the powers that be, see Christopher Rowland, "A Kingdom but Not as We Know It," *Ekklesia*, http://www.ekklesia.co.uk/node/8020; T. E. D. Troxell, "Christian Theory," *Journal for the Study of Radicalism* 7, no. 1 (2013): 37–59; Alexandre Christoyannopoulos, *Christian Anarchism: A Political Commentary on the Gospel* (Exeter: Imprint Academic, 2011).

[10] The issue of sovereignty has been addressed with attention to its historical background and the revival of political theology by Paul W. Kahn, *Sacred Violence: Torture, Terror, and Sovereignty* (Ann Arbor: University of Michigan Press, 2008); Paul W. Kahn, *Putting Liberalism in Its Place* (Princeton, NJ: Princeton University Press, 2005); Paul W. Kahn, *Political Theology: Four New Chapters on the Concept of Sovereignty* (New York: Columbia University Press, 2012); Paul W. Kahn, "Political Theology: A Response," *Political Theology* 13, no. 6 (2012): 751–61. On the theological relevance of this debate, see Luke Bretherton, "'Love Your Enemies': Usury, Citizenship and the Friend-Enemy Distinction," *Modern Theology* 27, no. 3 (2011): 366–94. William T. Cavanaugh, "Am I Impossible? A Political Theologian's Response to Kahn's Political Theology," *Political Theology* 13, no. 6 (2012): 735–40. Sovereignty is connected both theoretically and empirically to the manifestation of the sacred in the nation-state.

Bureaucratic and technological development has enhanced state capacity to make its claims effective in its capacity to reach into the life of the community, whether delivering social services or mobilizing for war. The twenty-first-century nation-state is qualitatively different from its sixteenth-century predecessors.[11] The pre-modern state was "in many crucial respects partially blind; it knew precious little about its subjects, their wealth, their landholdings and yields, their location, their very identity."[12]

Today, in the early twenty-first century, the state routinely reaches deep into the lives of individuals through enhanced technology and information processing. It can standardize, measure, centrally record, and monitor people's activities, their land, and their economic transactions with the capacity to match its authority to tax, conscript, and intervene to deliver public health and social welfare and to conduct police and electronic surveillance.[13] The Australian government's capacity to direct what people can spend their welfare payment on or to monitor their individual telecommunications demonstrates this substantial reconfiguring of the character and capacity of the state.

As that survey of the extended reach makes clear, the nation-state can attempt to remake much of social and physical reality, though the policy may prove ineffective

---

[11] See the comments by Sacks on the power of the state to reach directly into the life of communities. Jonathan Sacks, *The Politics of Hope* (London: Vintage, 2000), 68–69.

[12] James C. Scott, *Seeing Like a State: How Certain Schemes to Improve the Human Condition Have Failed* (New Haven, CT: Yale University Press, 1999), 2.

[13] Scott, *Seeing Like a State*, 2. The creation of equal citizenship had the consequence of undercutting the intermediary structures between the state and the individual and gave the state direct access to its citizens. See Scott, *Seeing Like a State*, 61n363.

or have disastrous outcomes. Such policy failure is most likely where there is a combination of unquestioned faith by those exercising power of the absolute rationality and desirability of their project, where the exercise of power is unaccountable, and where non-state institutions are unable to provide resistance.[14] That the nation-state is, in any unqualified sense, in the common-good business is a highly contestable proposition.[15] It may, on occasion, act with some relative degree of accountability; deliver services with varying levels of equity, efficiency, and effectiveness; and encourage some forms of civic virtue and human flourishing. Such achievements are worthwhile, though the condition of the poorest and most marginal within a nation-state is frequently occluded from view in both policy design and implementation.[16]

The nation-state has clearly emerged in the past century as a central repository of sacred value and loyalty.[17] Citizenship even in supposedly secular countries is tied to symbols and

---

[14] Scott, *Seeing Like a State*, 2.

[15] In Catholic Social Teaching, the state is necessary, natural, good, and limited, based on the social nature of humanity, and with the purpose of pursuing the common good. The teaching evidences a process of historical development in shifting accounts of the state through the various encyclicals. See Charles E. Curran, *Catholic Social Teaching 1891–Present: A Historical, Theological and Ethical Analysis* (Washington, DC: Georgetown University Press, 2002), 137–44. Theologians, by contrast, often conceive the "state" as unchanging in character assuming "that the state is natural and primordial." William T. Cavanaugh, "Killing for the Telephone Company: Why the Nation-State Is Not the Keeper of the Common Good," *Modern Theology* 20, no. 2 (2004): 244.

[16] A theologically informed account of the US context is provided in William Stringfellow, *My People Is the Enemy: An Autobiographical Polemic* (Eugene, OR: Wipf & Stock, 2005).

[17] See Carolyn Marvin and David W. Ingle, *Blood, Sacrifice and the Nation: Totem Rituals and the American Flag*, ed. Jeffrey C. Alexander and Stephen Seidman (Cambridge: Cambridge University Press, 1999).

rituals that express and reinforce devotion of individuals to the nation-state.[18] National identity "becomes one's primary loyalty, and that which separates one's nation from all others is highlighted."[19] The state, through the liturgies of civil religion,[20] has taken on a manifestly sacred character in which citizens may be called upon to kill, or be killed, on its behalf and at its behest.[21]

The Salvation Army and the State in Its Sacral Mode

The Salvation Army's experience of contracting to provide welfare and humanitarian support services for offshore asylum seekers reveals what can happen when a church-related agency engages with government operating in sacral mode. In late 2012, the Australian government announced a contract for the provision of welfare and support services for asylum seekers on Manus Island and Nauru processing centres with the Salvation Army, to run from February 2013 to January

---

[18] For a historical account of political thought behind the transfer of the sacred to the state, see Rosco Williamson, "The Sacred Stays Central: Agency and Transcendent Credibility in Early Modern Political Theories of Authority," *Political Theology* 16, no. 2 (2015): 159–75. On the sacred character of national symbolism in a secular guise, see Talal Asad, "French Secularism and the 'Islamic Veil Affair'," *The Hedgehog Review* 8, no. 1–2 (2006): 494–526.

[19] Cavanaugh, "Killing for the Telephone Company," 264.

[20] "The Liturgies of Church and State," in *Migrations of the Holy: God, State and the Political Meaning of the Church*, ed. William T. Cavanaugh (Grand Rapids, MI: Eerdmans, 2011), 115–22.

[21] Kenneth Stanley Inglis and Jan Brazier, *Sacred Places: War Memorials in the Australian Landscape*, 3rd ed. (Melbourne, VIC: Melbourne University Press, 2008).

2014, valued at $74.9m.[22] The Salvation Army had taken the initiative in approaching the government following the policy announcement through the office of the Minister for Immigration, offering to provide services for asylum seekers, having already been involved with community detention on the Australian mainland.

Major Brad Halse, as the government relations manager for the Southern Territory insisted that while the Salvation Army did not agree with the government's asylum seeker policy, it took the view that if the government is proceeding with the policy the relevant issue concerned the next best thing for the asylum seekers:

> The view of the Salvation Army at that time...was to have a group of people highly committed to maximise the very best out of a bad option for people so we felt that the church should be involved in that....There was a memorandum of understanding at that stage rather than a formal contract. Everything was being done on the run from the Department....The final shape of the contract and the restrictions in it were far less than what was originally mooted....There were things where we just said, "Well, we can't work on this basis"....The urgency of this thing, the speed with which it's happened, certainly framed our executive decision making process....We don't really like to work like that but it was always the principle that "Well, you know, here's a great need. There are people being sent there and nobody's really there to be able to look after their welfare needs, basic education, support," things like that and, you know, the overriding biblical principle for us is, "Well, there's a human need and can we meet it, do we

---

[22] For a well-documented account of the policy, its implementation, and its impact, see Madeline Gleeson, *Offshore: Behind the Wire on Manus and Nauru* (Sydney, NSW: University of NSW Press, 2016), 12–100.

have the resources, do we have a level of experience and expertise?"[23]

In the Army's perspective, the people sent to Nauru and Manus Island were fleeing dangerous and life-threatening situations, arriving traumatised and in need of care. During their stay in overseas processing centres the Army "was committed to providing care for these asylum seekers, regardless of politics or popularity."[24] According to Major Paul Moulds, the Army was there "because we care deeply for the plight and the situation of the asylum seekers and believe our presence can make and is making a difference."[25] The Army's decision to undertake this contract needs to be assessed against both its mission and identity and what actually happened on the ground in its delivery of that service.

As an international movement, the Salvation Army understands itself to be an evangelical part of the church universal, with a mission to preach the gospel of Jesus Christ and to meet human needs in his name without discrimination. The

---

[23] Major Brad Halse (Government Relations, Salvation Army Southern Territory), interview by Douglas Hynd, Blackburn, 20 February 2014.

[24] Salvation Army Eastern Territory, "Asylum Seekers & Refugees Factsheet," https://salvos.org.au/scribe/sites/auesalvos/files/Fact_Sheet_-_Asylum_Seekers_and_Refugees.pdf. On the full 2012 statement by the Army, see Salvation Army Australia Eastern Territory, "Salvation Army Statement on Involvement in Support to Asylum Seekers on Nauru and Manus Island," http://www.salvationarmy.org.au/Global/News and Media/news/2012/final-asylum-seeker-statement-sep-2012.pdf.

[25] Major Paul Moulds in evidence on "Migration Legislation Amendment (Regional Processing and Other Measures) Act 2012 and Related Bills and Instruments," Australia Parliamentary Joint Committee on Human Rights (Canberra, ACT: Hansard, 2012), https://parlinfo.aph.gov.au/parlInfo/search/display/display.w3p;query=Id A committees commjnt 46787736-005b-46df-94f5-4a707fa02cdb 0008.

work of the Army is about transforming lives, caring for people, making disciples, and reforming society. Starting from the recognition that God is always at work in the world, the Army values human dignity, justice, hope, compassion, and community. Yet, while the Army were there to provide humanitarian support to asylum seekers, the government detention centre was established to deter desperate people from seeking protection, through subjecting asylum seekers to intentionally cruel conditions.

The implementation of the contract by the Army suffered from inexperienced staff, poor preparation, and its inability to defend the asylum seekers' human rights.[26] The expedited implementation caused substantial difficulties. Screening of workers for skills and maturity, along with appropriate briefing and preparation was almost non-existent in the first round of placements. While questions were publicly raised about the consistency between the Army's commitments and mission and participation in a program that they were opposed to, the Army strongly defended its action:

> The Salvation Army has supported and endorsed the comments made by Amnesty International and the recent UNHRC report. We recognise conditions are harsh, and any comments that could be considered as "defending conditions" were simply truthful answers to questions regarding the adequacy of food and water. Our staff are working hard every day to give every asylum seeker access to education, vocational training, recreational and social

---

[26] Mark Isaacs, *The Undesirables* (Richmond, VIC: Hardie Grant Books, 2014), 8.

activities that will make the time awaiting the resolution of their asylum claims more meaningful and useful.[27]

The institutional environment created by government policy was one in which abuse of both asylum seekers and support staff became normalized. The management of the contract by the Australian government was undertaken in a way that enabled it to obfuscate its responsibility for the impact of the policy and to ignore reports from accountability agencies such as the Australian National Audit Office and the Australian Human Rights Commission.[28]

The Army defended its "realism" in accepting the contract as recognition of an electoral mandate by the government for the policy. It apparently viewed government policy in purely bureaucratic terms, assuming that contract provisions and the policy framework meant exactly what they said, rather than recognizing that operating in a sacral mode, the Australian government was prepared to do whatever it took to achieve its political ends. Crucial to the process by which the Army became an extension of the state in this contract is the fundamental logic of deterrence in the offshore processing policy. The policy of deterrence requires penalizing people, causing cruelty to some on the basis that such acts would save lives by deterring others from a dangerous sea journey.

If the state is prepared to call for its own citizens to sacrifice their lives to ensure its survival, we should not be surprised

---

[27] Major Paul Moulds, "No Sanction of Policy as Salvos Aid Asylum Seekers," *Sydney Morning Herald*, 24 December 2012, http://www.smh.com.au/federal-politics/no-sanction-of-policy-as-salvos-aid-asylum-seekers-20121223-2btec.html. On the criticism, see Bruce Haigh, "The Salvation Army Is a Branch of Government," *On Line Opinion: Australia's E-journal of Social and Political Debate*, http://www.onlineopinion.com.au/view.asp?article=15013.

[28] Gleeson, *Offshore*, 94–197.

when it is prepared to treat carelessly and even inhumanely those who are not its members, in a situation it describes as a threat to national borders and sovereignty,[29] a situation analogous to a state of war. Given the perception of threat by asylum seekers to the integrity of the state, a challenge to what is most sacred, it is no surprise that the humanity of asylum seekers would be ignored in the way they are treated. There was a wide gap between the official rhetoric of providing appropriate facilities and care for asylum seekers and the reality of detention as abusive and oppressive in defending the sacred. This permitted those responsible for implementing policy to engage in harsh treatment of those imprisoned, even if such treatment was not explicit in either policy or the contract. The Army was caught unaware of the full significance of the policy it was involved in implementing and became squeezed between its religious identity and humanitarian mission and the underlying abusive policy logic of deterrence and detention.

The Salvation Army was finally unable to assert, in anything more than a fragmentary way, its own mission, a practice of compassion and humanity against the pressures of government policy. The asymmetric exercise of power in the contract made it difficult for the Army to do anything except become an extension of the state. It was unable to effectively advocate on behalf of those it was trying to serve. Becoming an extension of the state was a result not only of the power relationship of the contract but also of the policy itself, shaped

---

[29] On the issue of borders, allegiances, and the identity of the church, see the theological discussion by Michael L. Budde, *The Borders of Baptism: Identities, Allegiances and the Church* (Eugene, OR: Cascade Books, 2011).

by the exercise of sovereignty and the sacred character of the state.

How Theology Found Its Way into Agency Decision Processes and What Difference It Makes

Agencies dealing with the state operating in its bureaucratic mode encounter a policy logic of a utilitarian calculus and a vocabulary at odds with commitments to human value, spiritual reality, and community formation. Employment-services contracting was initially characterized by a swing to a policy encouraging innovative, flexible service by non-government providers. The flexibility in the policy did not last long, however, with a shift back towards command and control contracting from the second round of contracts. Within less than a decade, this resulted in a form of service delivery emerging that differed little from the bureaucratic starting point in the Commonwealth Employment Service it was meant to replace.[30]

Applying a values/mission template to the contract decision-making process is a tactic an agency can use to ensure that the contracts it enters into meet its mission focus. Such a template provides an entry point for theology to make a difference

---

[30] On the employment services sector generally, see Mark Considine, Jenny M. Lewis, and Siobhan O'Sullivan, "Quasi-Markets and Service Delivery Flexibility Following a Decade of Employment Assistance Reform in Australia," *Journal of Social Policy* 40, no. 4 (2011): 811–33; Mark Considine, Siobhan O'Sullivan, and Phuc Nguyen, "Mission Drift?: The Third Sector and the Pressure to Be Businesslike; Evidence From Job Services Australia," *Third Sector Review* 20, no. 1 (2014): 87–107. On the impact on church-related agencies, see Wilma Gallet, "Marketized Employment Services: The Impact on Christian-Based Service Providers and Their Clients," *International Journal of Public Sector Management* 29, no. 5 (2016): 426–40.

to agency engagement with government. In the Catholic social welfare agencies' decision making about involvement or non-involvement in employment-services contracting, reference to Catholic Social Teaching (CST) played a significant role in the assessment and decision process.

The Catholic identity of the agencies was articulated with specific reference to CST as a benchmark for both program priorities and the way programs were delivered. From 1998 onwards, when the contracting began, about a quarter of the agencies in the Catholic network were involved in Job Network and its successor, Jobs Services Australia (JSA), contracts for mainstream employment services. The Personal Support Program (PSP) for disadvantaged jobseekers was much more popular with Catholic agencies as almost every agency in the network delivered it.[31] The contract for the Job Network involved tension between some elements of what it required compared to some Catholic agencies' understanding of their role and mission.

> While the agencies were very comfortable working with particularly disadvantaged job seekers, because that's their core business, they weren't very comfortable often dealing with job-ready job seekers or those that were less disadvantaged....They thought the most disadvantaged were their main priority....PSP was very popular, because it was largely about counselling most disadvantaged job seekers.[32]

The government's need for weekly performance reporting had enormous potential to distract agencies from their focus

---

[31] Phil Murray (Former National Manager, CSSA), interview by Douglas Hynd, Canberra, 24 January 2014.
[32] Murray, interview.

on the individual dignity of the person coming through the door.[33] As the obligations around compliance documentation and reporting increased, this reduced the ability of agencies to proceed in a way that respected individual dignity in the manner required by church teaching. Another point of tension between agencies and government policy was the tightening of activity test arrangements for people on allowances. There was a clash between this policy and the way some agencies interpreted the teaching of the church.

> The work for the dole program was actually banned at one stage by what was then the Catholic Social Welfare Commission and it recommended that agencies didn't do Work for the Dole and only one or two ever did. They loosened that up later on when some changes were made to that program, such as the introduction of training credits that made it a little more supportive of job seekers....The activity test was another part of that whole thing that they were never really comfortable with. They didn't like the idea of having to report clients for breaches.[34]

The policy trajectory towards a command and control form of contracting in employment services increasingly left contracting agencies unable to deliver the program in a way that embodied their mission, with the result that they saw themselves as becoming an extension of the state. For Peter Sellwood, director of Brisbane Centacare, over time employment-services contracting took on a character at odds with Brisbane Centacare's identity and mission with respect to the teaching in CST on the individual and his or her place in society. "For us it was

---

[33] Frank Quinlan (Former Executive Director, Catholic Social Services Australia), interview by Douglas Hynd, Canberra, 18 November 2013.
[34] Murray, interview.

very much about the dignity and respect that comes from being part of work and therefore being part of the community. The workplace is very much a community and if you're excluded from that then you're excluded from a whole range of things."[35]

As an example of policy language at odds with Sellwood's own ethical and theological commitments, he notes how the department wanted to focus on people as "just a pool of unemployed people that were an economic problem."[36] Reference to the "stock of unemployed" by the government and the department was also offensive. Sellwood recalled that when he was unemployed, and between jobs "I didn't see myself as 'stock'. I saw myself as someone that needed a job, who wanted a job and could offer something to an employer."[37]

Because the payment scheme within the contract was based on moving people into jobs, it included no incentive to pay attention to people with multiple issues who could not be quickly or easily placed. While the agency understood its work with the individual in more complex ways, they faced upfront costs in doing so with a low likelihood of getting a payment for successful job placement in anything but the long term. The Star ratings are an example of the axiom: all that matters is what is measured. If your Star ratings fell below the numbers needed to maintain the contract, the focus became increasing those numbers with the result that you could "take your eye off the ball in terms of the delivery of mission."[38] You could get caught up in behaviours that were not consistent with your

---

[35] Peter Sellwood (Director, Centacare, Archdiocese of Brisbane), interview by Douglas Hynd, Brisbane, 12 May 2014.
[36] Sellwood, interview.
[37] Sellwood, interview.
[38] Sellwood, interview.

mission because you were concerned with throughput. Even with respect to the PSP, a program much more closely aligned with the mission of the agency, it was possible to trace the same process of mission distortion. It "became very outcomes focused again, outcomes determined by the department, not outcomes determined by us and the clients we worked with."[39]

The decision of Brisbane Centacare to move out of employment-services contracting was a complex interaction between financial and mission factors. The original funding model was generous enough to "hide the challenges of delivering mission and being financially sustainable."[40] The possibility of maintaining this balancing act was undermined over time by the real term winding back of funding. The agency was squeezed on both the volume of work and the level of payment in the contract. That situation was not sustainable over the longer term and brought the conflict with its mission into clear focus for the agency. According to Sellwood, if you are running at a loss on a contracted program, it can only continue if the program is central to your mission. If it is central you will then find other funds to keep it going.

> That wasn't the case with employment....We weren't living out any mission because we were just a processing arm of government....There was no capacity for us to sit and work with a client and try and deal with the range of issues that might be confronting them, it was just get them in a job or you won't get paid....We had to be real about who we are and what we wanted to do and therefore we exited.[41]

---

[39] Sellwood, interview.
[40] Sellwood, interview.
[41] Sellwood, interview.

Theology Finding Its Way into Agency Processes

The role of theology in agency processes has not received a great deal of attention in the public policy and social sciences literature. By raising the issue of how an agency connected to the churches and its founding tradition in the interviews, I gained responses which brought theological questions into the discussion. The CEO of Anglicare Tasmania, the Rt. Rev. Chris Jones, reported that, in an ecumenical move, "I stole the Uniting Church's Faith Foundations document....I just crossed out Uniting Church and put Anglican Church....I went back out to our staff and said, this is what we're about."[42]

A variety of agencies developed orientation programs for staff, management, and board on the mission, identity, and underpinning theological commitments of the agency. The reality that an increasing majority of staff would not be Christians or familiar with the Christian tradition drove this tactic.[43] Anglicare Sydney responded to this challenge with a major investment in an education program for management centred around the mission and identity of the agency.[44] Catholic Social Services Victoria also put resources into this area by way of conferences and workshops for member agencies.

---

[42] Rt. Rev. Chris Jones (CEO, Anglicare, Tasmania), interview by Douglas Hynd, Canberra, 11 February 2014. While the *Faith Foundations* is a substantial theological statement with much to say about human flourishing, it has little to say in theological terms about the character of the state.

[43] Dr Stephen Judd, interview by Douglas Hynd, Sydney, 12 December 2013; Otto Henfling (CEO, Catholic Social Services, Parramatta Diocese), interview by Douglas Hynd, Parramatta, 29 January 2014.

[44] Peter Kell (Former CEO, Anglicare Sydney), interview by Douglas Hynd, Wollongong, 5 March 2014.

For Stephen Judd, CEO of HammondCare, the key question was one's alignment with the agency's identity and mission, because "the temptation for chief executives or general managers is to hire on the basis of skills and experience and then unfortunately having to fire on the basis of attitude or non-alignment."[45] Alignment is not necessarily a matter of being a Christian but one of being committed to the purpose of the organisation and being able to work for those purposes within its Christian identity.

> Our motivation statement, says why we do what we do and it says the words and deeds of Jesus is what inspires us...and because of this we believe that all people are worthy of dignity and respect....What I say in staff orientations is...[i]f you can't say that you believe that people are worthy of dignity and respect and compassion, even if you don't agree with me on where it comes from, go and do something else.[46]

The role played by leadership in owning and communicating the identity and founding story of the agency was key. Rev. Ray Cleary, reflecting on his time as CEO of Anglican agencies, explained that

> You have to be the narrator, you have to be the storyteller and you have to be able to speak to people where you're at....Most of my role is actually talking with staff, meeting with staff, listening to their stories, trying to respond to their story in a way that would give them confidence that their own role was significant and important in meeting the objectives of the organisation.[47]

---

[45] Judd, interview.
[46] Judd, interview.
[47] Rev. Ray Cleary (Former CEO, Anglicare Victoria), interview with Douglas Hynd, Melbourne, 5 December 2013.

Michael Yore, former CEO of Good Shepherd Youth and Family Services, also stressed the vital role of leaders in knowing and carrying the story of an agency. Leaders have to "have the capacity to tell the story in a way that is engaging, for young staff in particular who are totally disengaged from anything religious."[48] There is an inherent and inescapable tension in seeking to maintain identity. It involves treading a fine line between retreating into "some sort of Catholic ghetto, returning an organisation to a kind of defensiveness in the face of pluralism on the one hand, and the acceptance of assimilation by a secular society and the 'dumbing down' of organisational identity and mission."[49]

Sue Ash, CEO of UnitingCare West, affirmed that "we honour and connect with the faith base of the organisation that we are effectively and legally part of, and that's the Uniting Church. People at an executive level when they're recruited we really put them through the paces of what does that mean."[50] Agency identity is maintained through the role of the mission development leader who is on the executive of the agency. The role includes "connecting the agency to the church; connecting the church to the agency; and ensuring that there's a missional

---

[48] Michael Yore (Former CEO, Good Shepherd Youth and Family Services), interview with Douglas Hynd, East Melbourne, 23 May 2014. This issue has been the subject of substantial discussion; see Gabrielle McMullen and John Warhurst, eds., Listening, Learning and Leading: The Impact of Catholic Identity and Mission (Ballarat, VIC: Connor Court Publishing, 2014). See also Michael Yore, "Having an Impact: Do Social Services Shaped by Catholic Identity Make a Difference? A Catholic Social Services Victoria Occasional Paper" (2016), http://www.css.org.au/Portals/51/HAVING AN IMPACT/April2016.pdf.

[49] Yore, interview.

[50] Sue Ash (CEO UnitingCare West), interview with Douglas Hynd, Perth, 11 April 2014.

connection between the values and direction of the agency with the values and theology of the church."[51]

For Rockhampton Centacare, the theological significance of this governance arrangement is front and centre. "[T]he bishop really is the head of the church here and so he's the head of this organisation. And we take a lot of time making sure staff understand that they are a church worker....[W]e are the ministry of the bishop of the diocese."[52] Though the agency is 96 percent government funded, it nevertheless affirms its Christian identity in its statement of mission. The agency is called to share in the healing ministry of Jesus by providing professional community services to enhance the well-being of individuals and families. Under the heading of "Faith" on its website is the statement that "Centacare is a ministry of the Catholic Church. Our Mission is: to share in the healing ministry of Jesus....Most of all Centacare offers good news to all who experience some sense of poverty in their lives because Centacare offers Hope."[53]

To maintain the Catholic identity of the agency, "leaders in the organisation had to have some post-graduate qualification in leadership and Catholic identity. So we've done that course through ACU and that's part of the employment for the senior management."[54] A number of channels were used in communicating the Catholic identity to agency staff. Once a month the staff reflects on how their work relates to the mission.

---

[51] Ash, interview.

[52] Dr Ricki Jeffery (Director, Centacare, Rockhampton), interview with Douglas Hynd, Yepoon, 9 May 2014.

[53] It quotes from Luke 4:18 where Jesus takes up and reads a passage from Isaiah 6:12.

[54] Jeffery, interview.

We write a reflection on one of the gospels every Sunday and send that out first thing Monday morning, which says what's this gospel telling us and how does that relate to 2014, and issue a challenge in their space....It's not that we want people to turn into Catholics, but we actually say our values are based in the gospels, Catholic social teaching, social justice is part of our space. So we're continually giving some examples and reminders that that's who we are.[55]

Conclusion

"At the heart of any meeting between religious communities and the modern state is an encounter of epistemologies—theories of knowledge, the nature of truth and the sources and ultimate purpose of human flourishing."[56] It took some time for some church-related agencies in the shift to contracting to recognize the nature and importance of this encounter. It did, however, emerge over time. And in conversations with church-related agencies, theology was acknowledged to have had an important role in agency decision processes, in assisting and guiding their reflection on how their mission and ecclesial identity informed their engagement with the state. Getting their bearings from Scripture and various Christian theological traditions helped agency management and boards to query the default assumptions of a close linkage with the state. It allowed them to maintain a critical political stance with respect to government and to avoid becoming simply an extension of the state.

---

[55] Jeffery, interview.
[56] Francis Davis, "Editorial: Religion, Third Sector, Policy and Public Management," *Public Money & Management* 29, no. 6 (2009): 337–40.

Examining Mission Threat in a World of Competitive Tendering: Disability Employment Case Study

Brendan Long

The Research Question

The analysis presented here is both a work of social policy analysis and a work of public and practical theology. Using the conceptual framework of Catholic Social Teaching (CST), this chapter reflects on the issue of mission threat within a theological perspective. It unites this theological analysis with economic analysis concerning divergent incentive structures of for-profit, not-for-profit, and Christian providers. It analyses how these incentive structures interact with governmental regulatory structures in a competitive tendering context using disability employment as a case study.

Certainly, it belongs to government to structure tendering arrangements and the performance frameworks that may underpin them, in order to maximise a sought policy outcome at least cost. This is desirable economically. The experience in such tendering arrangements, however, in the social policy sphere in general and in the disability employment services area in particular, is that these forms of regulation tend to develop organically with continual refinement with every tendered contract renewal. This presents both a challenge and an opportunity for Christian social services providers. Christian social services providers interact with regulators to ensure not only that regulation and tendering models do not involve mission threat but also that they are sufficiently flexible to allow the specific theological charism of the charities' mission objectives to be fully recognised. This is the opportunity. The challenge is for Christian providers to do this in a way that meets government's social and fiscal objectives.[1]

The question of the impact of tendering on Christian charities is a vast topic and there are myriad different market and regulatory structures in different sectors. In recognition of this problem, the following focuses on the disability employment sector as a sectoral case study. This highlights how competitive tendering interacts with the divergent incentives faced by for-profit, general not-for-profit, and Christian social services providers. The research questions for the paper are as follows:

- What are the differential incentive structures facing for-profit providers and non-Christian and Christian not-for-profit providers in the regulated market of disability employment services and how do they interact with tendering decisions?
- How does a theological conception of mission direct the incentive structures facing Christian providers in the regulated market of disability employment services and how do they interact with tendering decisions?
- What is the evidence on performance of Christian charities relative to other providers in contracting arrangements on disability employment?
- As the government engages with the disability sector to reform tendering arrangements, can tendering arrangements be constructed in a manner which aligns with the mission of Christian charities?

---

[1] See A. Nevile, "Drifting or Holding Firm? Public Funding and the Values of Third Sector Organisations," *Policy & Politics* 38, no. 4 (2010): 531–46.

In a world of regulatory risk, it is hoped that this analysis will better equip managers of Christian social services organisations in resource allocation to sustain alignment of their Christian mission with their service delivery objectives. It is also hoped that the research will inform governmental policy to build a competitive tendering model that recognises and, as far as possible, respects the theological mission of Christian social services providers.

Mission Threat and Mission Drift

The concept of "mission drift" has entered the parlance of mainstream managers, military leaders, and social services CEOs. Its use in more secular contexts reflects the concern that the original goal of an enterprise has become captured by forces beyond its control. As a result, the goal begins to encompass wider concerns to the detriment of the original objective—the mission—of the activity first undertaken. Mission drift leads to a loss of focus on the original purpose pursued and can reach a point of crisis when this original purpose is lost or efforts to pursue it are fragmented.

In the sphere of social enterprises, managers of not-for-profit organisations understand mission drift in less lofty and more practical terms. Incorporating commercial approaches risks a compromise between the organisation's mission of social services delivery by causing a "drift" too far into a purely commercial approach. Such a compromise can affect organisational reputation and threaten donor support. It may also undermine the organization's culture and lead to a loss of focus on the social goals and policy purpose the agency has sought to achieve in service delivery.

For Christian social services providers, the mission risk can be understood in theological terms. Christian welfare organizations exist to pursue a charitable purpose inspired by the values of the gospel. These values are captured in Christ's understanding of his own mission, spoken in the synagogue of Nazareth (according to Luke 4:16-20) before he embarked on a short public career. To use contemporary parlance, it was something of a "mission statement":

> He went to Nazareth, where he had been brought up, and on the Sabbath day he went into the synagogue, as was his custom. He stood up to read, and the scroll of the prophet Isaiah was handed to him. Unrolling it, he found the place where it is written: "The Spirit of the Lord is on me, because he has anointed me to proclaim good news to the poor. He has sent me to proclaim freedom for the prisoners and recovery of sight for the blind, to set the oppressed free, to proclaim the year of the Lord's favour."

These words inspired a commitment of service from Christian's leaders like Caroline Chisholm, St Mary Mackillop, and a legion of less-known names. These individuals slowly built a system of social services delivery in this nation, which has now been largely absorbed into the complex governmental system of service delivery which is the Australian welfare system. Christian social services remain, however, a substantive part of this system in education, health care, aged care, and social services support—a manifold system of service delivery.

It is a brute fact that, to continue to function and pursue their theological mission, Christian social services providers have had to adjust their business models to pursue what is essentially a corporate model, meeting stringent demands of government regulation and competing for a share of this "market." Let us be clear, this is the current state of service delivery in the Australian welfare system—it is a market. It is not a natural market of the type one finds in its rawest form in the fruit and vegetable markets in major metropolitan areas, and where prices move quickly to clear the market. It is an artificially created market. The government tends to fix prices and often also fixes the quantity of the market though demanding and burgeoning regulation with strict penalties for noncompliance.

It is inevitable that these demands create risks when attempting to meet the theological goals of Christian social services providers. They are not in it for the money, which is usually heavily constrained by tight government contracts; they are in it to pursue their theological mission. The risks are many and varied. There is the risk that the effort devoted to regulatory compliance will deprive them of resources to fulfil their theological mission. Research funded by the ACNC has shown that this burden is increasing.[2] There is the risk that the missionary goals might be diverted due to the intent of government policy, that is, the policy does not align with the theological vision. There is the ultimate risk that the project will fail—the missionary objective will be lost because the Christian service provider loses government support and loses the critical tender. A squandering of spiritual capital can result—social capital is deployed for a spiritual purpose and implies an opportunity cost. This can lead to a cost in a theological opportunity—the lost capital could have been deployed to other worthy projects inspired by the

---

[2] Ernst & Young, "Research into Commonwealth Regulatory and Reporting Burdens on the Charity Sector: A report prepared for the Australian Charities and Not-for-profits Commission" (30 September 2014), http://www.acnc.gov.au/ACNC/Pblctns/Rpts/EY_Report/ACNC/Publications/Reports/EY_report.aspx.

theological purpose.[3] There is also the risk, of course, that the venture may fail due to poor management or fraud or serious noncompliance, a risk all providers face. In the face of these challenges there will inevitably be a measure of mission drift—where the theological objective is diverted or fragmented.

Christian social services providers identify this mission drift as a key concern and tend to question whether the benefits of competitive tendering outweigh these risks.[4] If mission drift is a significant concern, the question becomes one of when this concern reaches a critical juncture, a tipping point when mission drift risks mission failure. In the terminology used in this study, when this tipping point is approached, mission drift becomes mission threat. The essential question at stake here is as follows: does the process of competitive tendering arrangements contain a systemic bias which inherently constitutes mission threat, and if so, what are the origins of this systemic bias?

The following engagement of Christian social service providers in the disability employment sector in Australia provides a case study to evaluate this issue of mission threat. It builds on the author's experience as a representative of such agencies, as national manager of economics and employment at National Disability Services (NDS) for three years from 2011 to 2014. Like many sectors, disability employment is an area

---

[3] R. Putnam, "Bowling Alone: America's Declining Social Capital," *Journal of Democracy* 6, no. 1 (1995): 65–78.

[4] See various submissions to the 2015 Senate Community Affairs References Committee inquiry into the "Impact on Service Quality, Efficiency and Sustainability of Recent Commonwealth Community Service Tendering Processes by the Department of Social Services," https://www.aph.gov.au/Parliamentary_Business/Committees/Senate/Community_Affairs/Grants/Submissions.

where competitive tendering and government regulation has had a very significant impact on service delivery.

Why Focus on Disability Employment?

During my time as a national policy manager for providers of disability employment services at National Disability Services (a peak national body based in Canberra), the extent to which social service delivery was severely constrained, and in some cases incapacitated, by the proscriptive nature of a government tendering model and the extreme constraints of government regulatory requirements became apparent. Many of these providers are and were Christian charities. I say "were" because the tendering and regulatory environment was often so overbearing and so risky for providers that some of these committed charities simply failed. Much social capital was lost, and from a theological perspective, it might be suggested that "spiritual capital" was also lost. I wish to use the example of disability employment services providers' experience of the competitive tendering regime and associated regulation as a real-world example of mission threat.

Some of these providers are active or engaging with the National Disability Insurance Scheme (NDIS), an enormous social enterprise, and also face mission threat due to regulatory issues and pricing policies adopted under this scheme. So, some insights from the following analysis may be relevant for how Christian social service providers engage with the NDIS and how they are dealt with under the scheme.

Christian Mission in Social Services: The Perspective of CST

How Christian social services providers conceive their mission in theological terms informs how those providers offer services in pursuit of that mission. The broad methodological approach taken here uses CST as a theological framework to evaluate engagement in publicly funded service delivery from a Christian missionary perspective. Certainly, even within the Christian viewpoint, such a choice is not the only available approach. A natural law approach, or a biblically based viewpoint, could be adopted. The preference of approach may well be related to denominational theological commitments and preferred theological methods. Still, this caveat made, there is a good case for choosing CST as the basis for presenting a broad framework of ethical analysis to the specific problem of Christian social service engagement in a world of competitive tendering. This argument for adopting CST as the broad Christian moral lens is twofold. First, while obviously a corpus emanating from the Roman Catholic religious tradition, CST presents a framework based on biblical principles and attempts an ecumenical basis of interpretation, producing evolving analysis of the situation of all persons as they encounter the world in their lived situation, in their here and now. CST is quintessentially practical and public theology and is probably the strongest and loudest articulation of this stream of religious reflection. The second limb of this argument relates to the strident engagement of Pope Francis on economic issues, a commentary which has emerged as one of the central themes of Francis' leadership. As I have argued elsewhere, Francis presents a strong critique of economic institutions and processes based on CST.⁵ In *Evangelii Gaudium*, he observes how economic forces exacerbate the problem of social exclusion:

> Just as the commandment "Thou shalt not kill" sets a clear limit in order to safeguard the value of human life, today we also have to say "thou shalt not" to an economy of exclusion and inequality. Such an economy kills....Human beings are themselves considered consumer goods to be used and then discarded. We have created a "throw away" culture which is now spreading. It is no longer simply about exploitation and oppression, but something new.⁶

Who is being killed by the consumer culture that throws away things? It is living human beings who are killed—we kill others by treating them as mere objects of consumption in our participation in an economic system which makes people merely goods that can be discarded.

Laudato Si' develops a new approach to the relationship between Christian theology and central social and economic issues and is highly critical in tone and content of contemporary economic institutions. This positive and critical account derives from a strong positive message of the power of Christian spirituality to open a new way of approaching the complex discussion between theology and economics. It is an appeal to an economic asceticism that should be adopted for the sake of the common good.⁷ In both works, Francis promotes CST as

---

⁵ Brendan Long, "What Does Pope Francis' Emerging Approach to Economics Mean for Tax Policy in Australia?," *St Mark's Review*, no. 235 (2016): 44–56.

⁶ Francis, Apostolic Exhortation *Evangelii Gaudium* (Vatican City: Vatican Press, 2013), §53.

⁷ Francis, Encyclical Letter *Laudato Si'* (Washington, DC: United States Conference of Catholic Bishops, 2015), §222.

a necessary reflective lens to consider contemporary economic issues.

CST is an evolving dialogue that speaks not just to those who hold the broad Christian view but to the whole community of persons, to and for all voices in this changing world and its social and economic structures. While CST has developed through papal instruction since the turn of the nineteenth century and remains a key element of the teaching of the official Roman Catholic hierarchy, one of its objectives is building a constructive and ongoing conversation between those who hold a particular religious perspective and the wider community who, on the whole, do not. The essential focus is on social reform. CST is not a body of work aimed at propounding theological propositions per se but is more an interpretive ethical framework proceeding from a broad set of values developed from a Catholic interpretation of the fundamental Christian message as applied to real-world policy concerns.

Here we immediately encounter an analytical problem: how might one apply CST as a generic Christian ethical framework to show how a Christian approach to mission affects decisions in the concrete world of government tendering for contracts—a very technical mundane activity? The proposed approach is as follows: the three principal elements of CST are taken as a basis for identifying the broad philosophical approach Christian organisations might adopt in deciding to engage in Christian social service activity. These primary concepts are (1) the notion of the common good, (2) the principle of solidarity, and (3) the preferential option for the poor. When seen in union, these principles provide an established analytical tool for the practical and public theologian to come to evaluation of a range of ethical concerns.

The CST corpus is substantial and developing, and there are many attempts to summarise its core features.[8] The US Conference of Catholic Bishops gathered an influential summary document of its key political elements,[9] and there is a *Compendium of Catholic Social Thought* issued by the Pontifical Council for Justice and Peace.[10] As with any Christian paradigm, CST presents an understanding of the human person in social life based on the Golden Rule: love your neighbour as yourself (Matt 22:39). This altruistic personal view is applied to the level of social concern or social policy in CST. To love others as oneself means to value their needs as we value our own and to engage in social reforms that create societies where this love and respect of the full dignity of all persons is celebrated, defended, and fostered. Respect for this dignity involves the whole person, not just a legal defence of fundamental human rights, but also calls for social and economic empowerment and especially the alleviation of poverty.

CST is concerned with the pursuit of the common good. The welfare of a community is integral to the welfare of the individual—they exist as twin principles which reinforce each other. The pursuit of charity, of service, of a socially just society, enhances the individual morally and spiritually and builds a community of justice from the bottom up. Under this principle,

---

[8] See J. Coleman, ed., *One Hundred Years of Catholic Social Thought: Celebration and Challenge* (Maryknoll, NY: Orbis Books, 1991), or T. Massaro, *Living Justice: Catholic Social Teaching in Action*, 2nd ed (Lanham, MD: Rowman and Littlefield, 2012) as examples.

[9] Task Force on Catholic Bishops and Catholic Politicians, *Readings on Catholics in Political Life* (Washington, DC: USCCB Publishing, 2006).

[10] Pontifical Council for Justice and Peace, *Compendium of the Social Doctrine of the Church* (Washington, DC: USCCB Publishing, 2005).

we are called to live "with others" and "for others." The common good, in fact, can be understood as the social and community dimension of the moral good.[11]

A just society respects the dignity of all individuals who then work together in harmony for mutual good. The pursuit of the common good is the task of enhancing the "sum total of social conditions which allow people, either as groups or as individuals, to reach their fulfillment fully and more easily."[12] It is not a utilitarian viewpoint where the social good or rules to enhance it are pursued in some great social cost/benefit calculus. Rather, it calls on the individual to value the welfare of all as much they value their own welfare and refuses to trade off aspects of the dignity of one to serve the good of the many. To the contrary, it insists that the good of all is only enhanced by respecting in all ways the rights and dignity of each person. The common good is enhanced when we see wealth and economic means as shared: owned by individuals but directed equitably for the pursuit of the welfare of all.

"Solidarity" is a further key principle of CST. There are two elements to this view: a personal level of commitment and a higher level of national and international commitment which speaks to the policy community. The latter is derived from the former. A just society is built on the moral relations of individuals who form a community of justice. It is not a top-down model where policy flows from an ivory tower. At the personal level, the principle of solidarity calls on all people to identify with the needs of others in their personal struggles, to take their side and to shoulder their yoke. We are called

---

[11] *Compendium of the Social Doctrine of the Church*, §164.
[12] "Pastoral Constitution on the Church in the Modern World, Gaudium et Spes," in *Vatican Council II: The Conciliar and Post Conciliar Documents*, ed.

to bear personally their pain, at least in some measure, by seeking to engage, encourage, and support them. The principle of solidarity seeks to foster a desire to share the experience of those who suffer. When this occurs, a heightened awareness of our mutual interdependence will naturally develop.

At the level of a society, this sense of solidarity leads to a commitment to respect the dignity of persons; to enhance their welfare, including their economic welfare; to encourage a fairer distribution of wealth; and to make a serious attempt to combat poverty. This sense of mutual collaboration for the good of all fosters a culture which seeks social improvement and builds social cohesion. In the words of Pope John Paul II,

> [T]he solidarity that we propose is the path to peace and at the same time to development...is inconceivable unless the world's leaders come to recognize that interdependence in itself demands the...transformation of mutual distrust into collaboration. This is precisely the act proper to solidarity among individuals and nations.[13]

This high level of analysis finds a very critical edge in a specific doctrine or ideal: the preferential love or option for the poor. The challenge it issues to policymakers lies in recognising that the needs of the poor and socially marginalised are so pressing that they should enjoy the first claim on the resources of government. This 1987 call by Pope John Paul II to leaders of nations remains relevant today:

> One of the themes of the Church's teaching is love or preference for the poor....[T]his preference for the poor must embrace...the hungry, the homeless, those in medical

---

[13] John Paul II, Encyclical Letter *Sollicitudo rei socialis* (30 December 1987), http://w2.vatican.va/content/john-paul-ii/en/encyclicals/documents/hf_jp-ii_enc_30121987_sollicitudo-rei-socialis.html, §39.

or other need, and above all those without hope of a better future. Our daily life as well as our decisions in the economic and political fields must be marked by these realities.[14]

CST interrogates how we might share deeply in each other's lives, in a spirit of solidarity with those who suffer, focusing specially on the needs of the economically and functionally marginalised for the sake of the common good. CST stresses the fundamental interconnectedness of our lives and the sense of co-suffering and co-participation in the travails of others. CST is an altruistic philosophy based on the Christian ideal of "agape" love: a sense of giving to others and sharing their burdens as the basic inspiration of life with a shared good and a sense of confidence in the capacity of programs of social justice.

The CST Perspective on Incentive Structures Facing Christian Social Services Providers

The central challenge CST poses to Christian social services providers concerns the alignment of their mission with the pursuit of the common good. This missionary goal influences the way Christian organisations operate. In Christian social service provision, CST calls for practical Christian action to serve those in need, acts of altruistic love based on the Golden Rule, a self-sacrificing "agape" love. It values the intention to serve those in need as the primary goal, driven by the desire for the common good, inspired by a decision to take a position of solidarity with those who are in need, and focusing on those in greater need preferentially over those in less need. These

---

[14] *Sollicitudo rei socialis*, §42.

are the incentive structures for the Christian social service provider called for by CST.

The incentive structures for other providers are different. The for-profit provider is a commercial organisation which will operate under the normal incentive structures faced by the market. The incentive structures for non-Christian not-for-profits will be different again. They will share some of the altruistic incentive structures of Christian providers but with probably less intensity as they are not inspired as directly by the "agape" perspective of love—self-sacrifice.

It may be possible to present a stylised form of these differential incentive structures within the context of standard microeconomic analysis, albeit in a rudimentary form.1 The basic model is that of the for-profit provider. Here the incentive structure is simply to maximise net revenue from the contract, optimising output (the level and type of service delivery) to minimise costs.

Let O (for output) be the level of services delivered.

Let C be the cost of delivery of the service for any given level of O.

Assuming the price per O is given by government in a fixed-price contract, we have a price per unit of output called "p." Let us also assume that demand is specified by the terms of the government contract so that we have a simple problem of choosing the optimal level of output O. C is a function of O—costs are a function of output usually decreasing as O increases due to increasing returns to scale of O. This means that $C(O)$ is monotonic decreasing in economic parlance: costs fall as output rises.

Revenue (R) for the social services provider is simply $R = p(O - C)$.

The optimal solution is to maximise output to the point where the marginal cost per unit (the extra cost per unit of increasing output) equals p.

Max R occurs when $d[C]/d[O]=p$.

Or, in plain English, where the additional cost per unit of output equals the fixed unit price set by government.

This model assumes any fixed costs are built into the unit price and there is no incentive to cross-subsidise from one line of output to other services. This is an assumption adopted for simplicity, and in fact there is often a process of cross-subsidisation in place called "overs and even" in the welfare sector where less profitable service lines are subsidised for reasons of mission by more profitable service lines. Accounting for this real-world situation would require a quite complicated multi-product model which would move the analysis away from an essentially theological and socio-scientific paper to a technical economic work.

The not-for-profit provider is likely to operate under a similar incentive structure but with some differences. As the provider does not need to return a market rate of return on capital invested, their cost structures may be lower, so they may be able to offer a higher output level or allow for "carrying" some less efficient operations for altruistic reasons and still cover costs. They may tend to offer a higher level of services closer to the point where the average cost approaches the fixed (see chart 1 below).

The for-profit provider will offer the service up to a point where the marginal financial benefit of providing an extra service equals the fixed per-unit price of providing the service.

So, the provider will stop providing the service when marginal costs equal the fixed per-unit price. Terms of the contract may restrict capacity of the service provider to reduce service levels below agreed thresholds, but, in essence, the for-profit service provider has a strong incentive to deliver services at a level driven by cost functions and the price level set by government. It is assumed that demand is sufficient to meet the service level, which is usually the case in most contractual arrangements with government. The non-Christian not-for-profit provider will behave in similar fashion but may tolerate a less ruthless calculation of the optimal service level to maximise profit and accept an outcome closer to a break-even position for altruistic reasons: more output with a lower return.

This economic paradigm of service delivery is not, however, consistent with the goals of mission inspired by CST. The critical theological issue from the CST perspective lies in denying the Christian organisation engaged in social service delivery the reduction of service to a form of utilitarian calculus governed by the best way to maximise a stated objective measured in purely a commercial sense: how to get the best value from the contract in terms of outcomes. CST says that the service provider offers a service to pursue the common good, expressing solidarity with those in need and directed to a preferential option for the poor—the needy. It further argues that the service should be offered to all in need according to the capacity of the organisation to meet that need. The organisation should maximise its efficient service delivery to those in need even beyond the most profitable output level specified in equations. O, the service delivery level, should take place until the venture becomes loss making. This is not when the marginal unit of service delivery equals the fixed price but at the higher level of output when average cost equals the fixed price. Beyond this level, total costs would exceed the total revenue and the business is loss making. CST does not necessarily call for a service provider to make losses as this would threaten the missionary goal originally sought.

So, we have here in this simple model a conflict between the economic goal and the missionary goal of the Christian service provider. The former calls for a level of service delivery set at marginal cost; the latter, a model closer to average cost. Mission calls on the provider to do more than is in their economic interests to pursue. If they follow CST they will not do as well against performance measures per unit set by government. They will offer more services, services exceeding the output level most efficiently offered under their cost structures, in order to meet the demands of service required by Christian mission. They will go "the extra mile" (Matt 5:41), do more than what the rational economist or the chief accountant would recommend. They must do this for the sake of the "agape love" which is their Christian mission. The problem is illustrated in the graph that follows.

Chart 1: A very basic graphical representation of differential pricing strategies of for-profit, not-for-profit, and Christian social services providers.

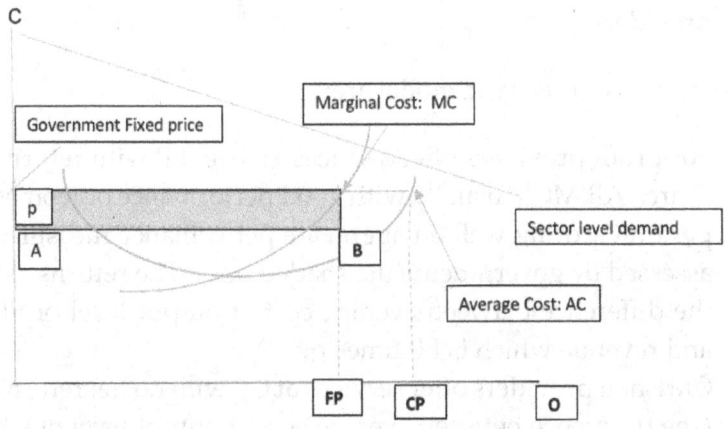

The above graph presents a stylised description of the market for social services. There are some essential features:

- The market for social services is created by government and is constrained by the government's budget constraint. Demand exceeds the fixed price that government can afford to pay for.
- For-profit providers still seek to offer services at marginal cost which is what they would do in a competitive market.
- Christian social services offer services at average cost, more services at a higher cost, due to the constraint of the "agape" mission perspective.

- Non-Christian not-for-profits offer a level of services between that offered by Christian social providers and for-profit providers.
- The model assumes similar cost structures between all providers.

The results of this basic model are:

- For-profit providers offer services at level FP with returns at area AB'MC'P usually with good performance outcomes per unit scoring well on aggregate performance measures assessed by government (the shaded box). The returns are the difference between average cost at output level of FP and revenue which is FP times p.
- Christian providers offer services at CP with no net returns (the difference between average cost at output level of CP and revenue which is CP times p=0).
- Not-for-profit non-Christian providers are the halfway house between for-profit and Christian providers with returns less than for-profit providers.

According to this stylised model, for-profit providers target output to that level which is economically efficient, offering a lower level of output but thereby capturing economic rent. Christian providers, by comparison, make no economic rent by offering services at a level which is just sufficient to cover costs in order to offer more services as demanded by their mission. The for-profit providers act to get the "cream" from the contract that Christian providers are not willing to seek because of their Christian commitments.

There are clearly some deficiencies with this simple model. It suggests that Christian and not-for-profit providers would offer a higher level of output than for-profit providers. There is no evidence for this, however, and Christian providers are likely to face a higher cost structure than for-profits with a higher cost of financing. Nevertheless, the simple model has the benefit of outlining the differential incentive structures facing different providers. Christian and not-for-profit providers will tend to offer services to the extent that they can afford to in pursuit of altruistic goals. For-profit providers will be more judicious about the level of service offering and target service delivery in any market segment that allows for greatest net revenue. This model is essentially a traditional natural monopoly model. It occurs when market prices are too high to provide for any normal private sector market to exist and the service can operate only with a government subsidy delivered for a social policy objective.

Analysis of Tendering Outcomes in Disability Employment

This generic model can be applied to the situation of service delivery in disability employment services. Some discussion of this tendering arrangement is warranted. Disability employment services have been offered to a range of providers under a competitive tendering model for over a decade. The tendering arrangements in place are now subject to review. One expected recommendation includes moving away from a tendering arrangement based on services offered in a strictly defined geographical area called the Employment Service Area (ESA) and towards a model less prescriptive in terms of government regulation. This will offer providers greater choice in terms of their service delivery model. Previously, contracts were offered at ESA level at a fixed price based on a mix of fixed service fees and outcome payments when persons employed achieved milestones in duration of employment (thirteen weeks, twenty-six weeks, or fifty-two weeks). Performance was assessed under a strict analysis of outcomes achieved subject to sophisticated regression analysis to control for the characteristics of service recipients and the economic conditions in the ESA. This led to a complex Star Rating system (one to five stars) which informed decisions on tendering at ESA level. Generally, only outcomes above the median outcome (midpoint of the three stars cohort) would secure funding. This performance regime is likely to continue in some form, though it is also now under review.

The Star Ratings system examines how measured performance varies between different provider types. Measured performance, of course, is just a stylised statistical approach to performance and so not necessarily a measure of real performance. Ann Nevile and Brendan Long, in their recent analysis, demonstrate that the Star Ratings often fail to capture the impact of differential service quality.[15] Star Ratings are produced every three months. This analysis considers the June 2017 and September 2017 datasets. Looking at Star Ratings in any quarterly period only provides a snapshot assessment of performance. The inclusion of two quarterly datasets is included to mitigate this deficiency.

In the following charts, N (light grey) refers to not-for-profit providers, P (dark grey) to for-profit providers, and C (solid black) to Christian providers.

---

[15] Ann Nevile and Brendan Long, "Beyond the Stars: A New Performance Management Approach for Disability Employment Services" (ARC Linkage Grant Report, 2016).

Table 1: June 2017 Star Ratings for DES providers by site and category of service delivery

	Number of Sites by Star Ratings and New Unrated Sites						Grand Total
	1	2	3	4	5	New Sites	
N	208	326	678	180	205	72	1,669
P	141	150	400	99	136	71	997
C	19	18	56	6	10	6	115
	Proportion of sites by Star Ratings						Mean Rating
N	12.46%	19.53%	40.62%	10.78%	12.28%	4.31%	2.90
P	14.14%	15.05%	40.12%	9.93%	13.64%	7.12%	2.93
C	16.52%	15.65%	48.70%	5.22%	8.70%	5.22%	2.72

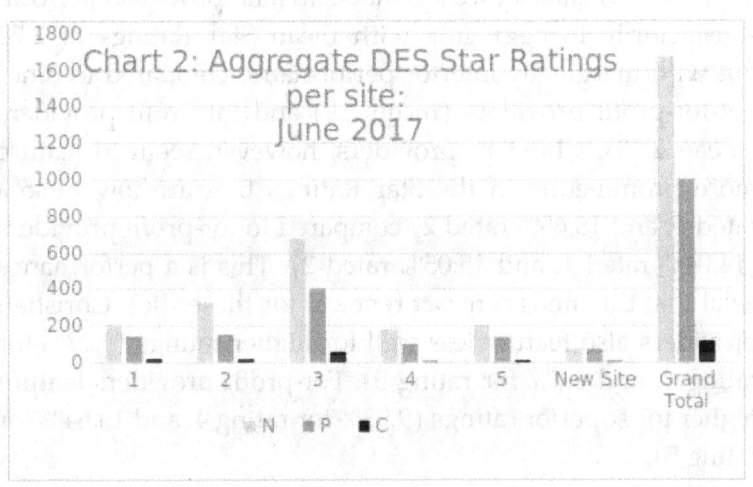

Chart 2: Aggregate DES Star Ratings per site: June 2017

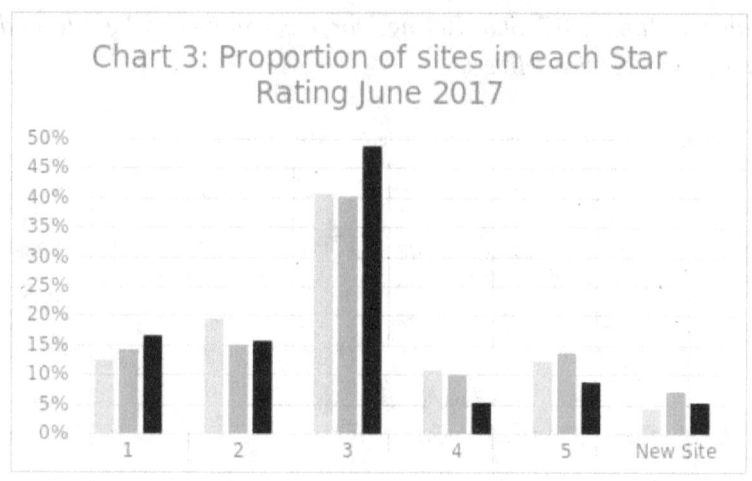

The data reveals some interesting conclusions. Looking at the June 2017 dataset we see that Christian providers perform satisfactorily in aggregate with mean Star Ratings of 2.72 but with marginally inferior performance compared to other not-for-profit providers (mean 2.9) and for-profit providers (mean 2.93). Christian providers, however, seem to feature more prominently in the Star Ratings that are low (16.5% rated 1, and 15.65% rated 2) compared to for-profit providers (14.04% rated 1, and 15.05% rated 2). This is a performance level that threatens contract renewal for these sites. Christian providers also feature less well for higher ratings (5.22% for rating 4, and 8.7% for rating 5). For-profit providers feature higher for superior ratings (9.93% for rating 4, and 13.64% for rating 5).

Table 2: September 2017 Star Ratings for DES providers by site category of service delivery

	Number of Sites by Star Ratings and New Unrated Sites						
	1	2	3	4	5	New Sites	Grand Total
N	201	329	643	201	208	63	1,645
P	112	189	385	110	150	72	1,018
C	23	29	44	3	10	6	115
	Proportion of sites by Star Ratings						Mean Rating
N	12.22%	20.00%	39.09%	12.22%	12.64%	3.83%	2.93
P	11.00%	18.57%	37.82%	10.81%	14.73%	7.07%	3.00
C	20.00%	25.22%	38.26%	2.61%	8.70%	5.22%	2.52

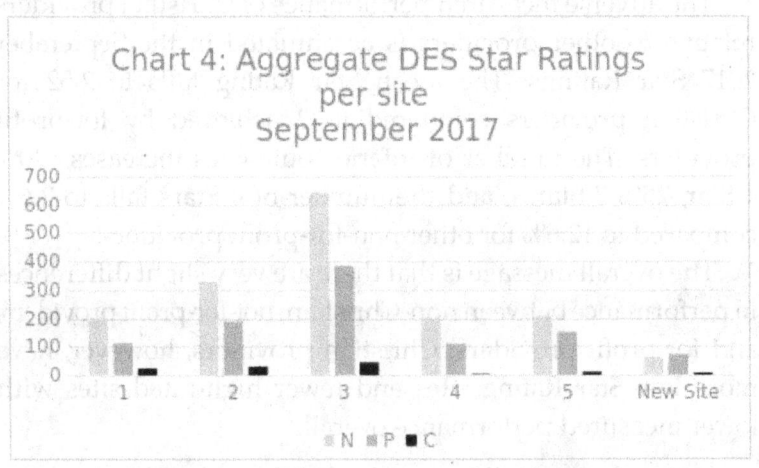

Chart 4: Aggregate DES Star Ratings per site September 2017

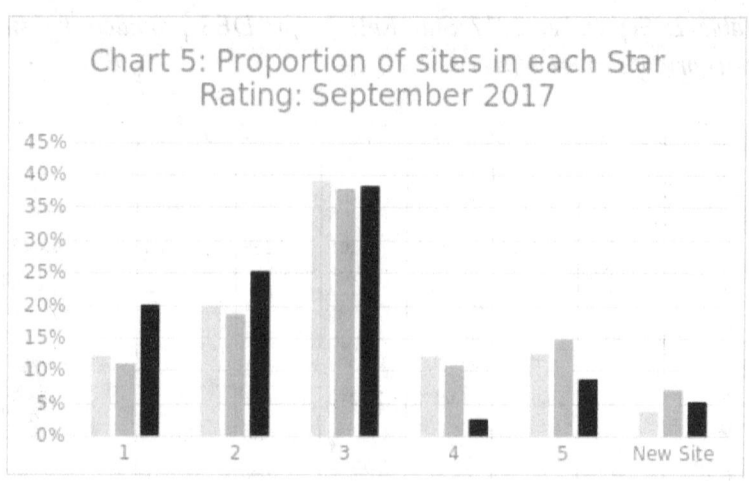

The adverse measured performance of Christian providers relative to other providers is accentuated in the September 2017 Star Ratings. The mean Star Rating falls to 2.52 for Christian providers compared to 3 achieved by for-profit providers. The number of inferior outcomes increases (20% 1 Star, 25% 2 Stars), and the number of 4 Stars falls to 2.6% compared to 12.6% for other non-for-profit providers.

The overall message is that there are very slight differences in performance between non-Christian, not-for-profit providers, and for-profit providers. Christian providers, however, have more low Star Rating sites and fewer high-rated sites with lower measured performance overall.

Conclusions on the Impact on Mission on Competitive Tendering in Disability Employment

Why do Christian providers perform worse overall? This analysis does not interrogate the various elements of the management practices of Christian social services providers and the underlying cost structures of their social enterprises. The basic model of economic incentives provided above and the theological framework of CST as presented above may explain this outcome, at least in part.

The generic incentive structures for Christian social services providers perhaps explains the measured outcome of relatively inferior performance under the strictures of the DES performance framework as it currently stands. The basic model presented above in chart 1 suggests that Christian providers seek to offer services close to average cost rather than a level of service delivery close to marginal cost that for-profit providers offer. It is not a free market as government sets the price and regulates access to the market based on a fixed-price contracting model. This model suggests that Christian providers tend to be more willing than for-profit providers to offer services to more difficult DES clients. They are more willing to take on higher-need clients, such as those with mental illness. As a consequence, they will be more open to taking clients with less chance of achieving an employment outcome. This would suggest a higher cohort of clients with more challenging conditions, and so greater difficulty in beating the average of measured performance under the DES performance framework. It is also likely that Christian social services providers will have a reduced cohort of outperforming sites. This is exactly what the data shows.

In effect, the data suggests that Christian social services providers are less likely to engage in "creaming" and so less likely to exit a difficult client as quickly as possible. The government, as architect and defender of the scheme, would argue that the DES scheme does not allow providers to "cream" the pool of DES clients and is required to take clients referred to it by Centrelink. The history of the operation of employment schemes in Australia suggests, however, that such constraints are not as tight as scheme advocates contend. The data presented in this analysis tends to support this conclusion.

The DES case study supports the conclusion that Christian social providers face a real tension between mission and performance under government tendering. In fact, performance in mission appears to be at the expense of performance under the contracting arrangement. The presented analytical model of incentives aligns with the theological model of missionary goals under a broad CST interpretive framework. This DES case study presents a real-world example of mission threat. This flows directly from a conflict between the missionary objective of service delivery to those in need in pursuit of the common good, on the one hand, and the structures of government contracting with a tight regulatory performance framework, on the other. The data supports a conclusion, at least in the area of the DES case study, that the requirements of the competitive tendering arrangements threaten the mission of Christian social services providers operative in the sector.

Wider Implications for Christian Mission and Government Tendering

While highlighting the specific case of disability employment providers, this analysis may provide insight into the broad problem faced by Christian social services providers. In order for them to be true to their mission, these providers will naturally be inclined to offer services at a level which is inspired by a generous "agape love" perspective, to offer what they can to those they encounter focusing primarily on their needs rather than a purely commercial decision-making approach. This commercially focused approach is likely to be stringent on service delivery, focusing always on the bottom line and requirements of performance targets set by government which increasingly wants more outcomes from less resourcing. These two worldviews, that of "agape love" by the Christian service provider and the commercial approach typified by the for-profit providers, seem to be necessarily in conflict at the most fundamental philosophical level.

The question is whether this conflict can be managed within a competitive tendering model. It is an open question. If government insists on subordinating the missionary objectives of Christian social service providers to overarching regulatory goals, threatening these goals, then the CST perspective outlined above would suggest that the common good is enhanced by an amicable divorce. Christian social service providers would opt out of government tendering and direct their missionary inspiration to other endeavours. Yet much social and spiritual capital, so painfully accumulated by over a century of loving service, would be squandered in such an outcome! Informal networks of service delivery built over many years would be lost for the sake of a regulatory objective. This would be a public policy approach that is self-defeating because the goals of the public policy program seek the very objectives that Christian social service providers are committed to serving. Such an outcome would constitute a significant failure of public policy.

Government and the Christian social services sector need to enter into a genuine dialogue that allows Christian missionary goals to be defended and celebrated by government. Certainly, there is always the need to measure performance and jealously guard the public purse to deliver the best outcomes for taxpayers. In principle, such a consensus position should be achievable, but it cannot be achieved if government fails to recognise that Christian social service providers have differential incentive structure to other providers. Government should be cognisant of the goals of Christian mission when it sets performance targets under government contracts. Flexibility in such arrangements could tolerate the differential incentive structures faced by for-profit, not-for-profit, and Christian providers. This may be achievable by building into the contracting model a measure of tolerance for the "agape love" perspective of providers who seek to offer services at a level not necessarily consistent with maximising outcomes under performance measurement approaches which reward providers who always beat the mean of measured performance. It is argued here that such performance frameworks struggle to recognise or reward the generosity of spirit which lies at the heart of Christian mission.

The alternative is that Christian providers may substantially scale back involvement with government to reduce threats posed to their mission. In the end, this would be a lose-lose situation for all parties and involve higher costs to government as activating Christian "agape love" in social service delivery probably reduces costs to government relative to government offering these services itself. This is the question for social policy makers in Australia: do we want a cold, commercially driven model, a corporate model, or do we value the commitment that Christian charities offer? Do taxpayers want Christians to deploy their altruistic motivations to pursue the common good? Though this is a choice for public policy, the motivations deployed by Christian social service providers, inspired by a framework like CST, have an inherent social value. They are more committed to the public policy goals behind government programs than many other providers. If this commitment is not valued, Christians will deploy their "agape love" in other ventures. Unless one is a complete secularist, such an outcome does not seem to resonate with a commitment to the common good of Australians.

Together We Stand: The Need for the Church to Unite in the Face of Marketisation of Human Services

Mark Zirnsak

The Rise of Neoliberalism

One argument which has manifest influence over our current society and, indeed, within international discourse is that of neoliberalism. This is an ideology that has, at its heart, the imposition of unrestrained markets in every aspect of our lives and society, the protection of private property, and small authoritarian government to enforce their imposition on the whole of society.[1] Imposing "economic freedom" is achieved through active policy interventions by government to remould institutions, state agencies, and individuals in ways that are compatible with the "free" market ethos and that are amenable to economic measurement. Government is therefore a powerful instrument of neoliberalism, though also an object of its constant critique, which is one of neoliberalism's many contradictions.[2]

Neoliberalism as an ideology is anti-Christian, due to its prioritisation of private wealth accumulation over the

---

[1] David Harvey, *A Brief History of Neoliberalism* (Oxford: Oxford University Press, 2005), 2.
[2] William Davies, *The Limits of Neoliberalism* (London: Sage, 2014), 5–6.

well-being of all. In Acts 4:32-35, the early Christians describe a society where all are provided for according to their need.

While neoliberalism is a broad movement, in reality its implementation has been to the detriment of the social majority. Neoliberalism is fuelling the rampant growth in inequality, both globally and locally, to the extent that even its traditional supporters (the OECD, the IMF, and the World Bank) have begun to express concern.[3] Neoliberalism has provided an environment in which executives can increase their pay at a much higher rate than the people who work for them, with higher levels of unemployment and the growing dominance of the financial sector over the rest of the economy and society.[4]

Neoliberalism came to prominence in the 1970s due to a confluence of social, political, and economic factors.[5] Freedom and individualism animated the student movements that swept the world in 1968—from Paris to Chicago to Bangkok and Mexico City.[6] The 1960s saw the rise of postmodernism, which questioned what was "normal," "true," "superior," or "just."[7] In a world where we cannot agree on what is "good" and what is "bad" because everything is a matter of personal or cultural perspective, measurement offers a solution. More

---

[3] See, for example, "OECD Forum 2015: Income Inequality in Figures," http://www.oecd.org/forum/issues/oecd-forum-2015-income-inequality-in-figures.htm; Era Dabla-Norris et al., Causes and Consequences of Income Inequality: A Global Perspective (IMF, 2015), https://www.imf.org/external/pubs/ft/sdn/2015/sdn1513.pdf; "Inequality and Shared Prosperity," http://www.worldbank.org/en/topic/isp

[4] William Davies, *The Happiness Industry* (London: Verso, 2015), 144.

[5] Harvey, *A Brief History of Neoliberalism*, 1.

[6] Harvey, *A Brief History of Neoliberalism*, 5.

[7] Davies, *The Happiness Industry*, 145.

is better than less, and to grow is to progress.[8] Neoliberalism was able to combine this valuing of growth with the value of freedom.

One of the founders of the current wave of neoliberalism, economist Milton Friedman, saw no problem in travelling to Chile in the spring of 1975 to advise the brutal dictatorship of General Pinochet.[9] The authoritarian nature of neoliberalism was shown more recently during the US occupation of Iraq, after the overthrow of the dictatorship of Saddam Hussein. On 19 September 2003, Paul Bremer, head of the Coalition Provisional Authority, issued decrees requiring the full privatisation of all public enterprises, full ownership rights by foreign corporations of Iraqi businesses, full repatriation of foreign profits, the opening of Iraq's banks to foreign control, and the elimination of nearly all trade barriers.[10]

While classical liberalism treats the "economic," "social," and "political" as separate spheres, each with their own discrete modes of evaluation, neoliberals evaluate all institutions and spheres of conduct according to a single economic concept of value. In doing so, neoliberals abandon the notion that the social and the public exists as something separate from the limits of commercial exchange.[11]

According to the neoliberal view of the world, human beings are constantly making cost-benefit trade-offs in pursuit of their interests. Caring for children, socialising with friends, getting married, going to church, designing a welfare program, and giving to charity were previously conceived as social and ethical considerations ritualised in faith. These activities

---

[8] Davies, *The Happiness Industry*, 146.
[9] Davies, *The Happiness Industry*, 146.
[10] Harvey, *A Brief History of Neoliberalism*, 6.
[11] Davies, *The Limits of Neoliberalism*, 21.

are now reconceived to become calculated strategies for the maximisation of private gain. This psychological model is known as "price theory," and neoliberals see no limit to its application.[12]

Led by the thinking of British economist Ronald Coase, one branch of neoliberal thinking has come to reject the idea that competition, run according to certain principles of fairness to prevent the distortion of monopolies, is desirable. Coase argued that markets are never perfectly competitive in actuality, so the categorical distinction between a market that "works" and one that "fails" is an illusion generated by economic theory. According to Coase, an economist should ask whether there is good evidence that a specific regulatory intervention in the market by government will make everyone better off overall. And by "everyone" he includes the party that is to be regulated. This, in effect, means that policy is to be directed by statistical data on aggregate human welfare alone and without reference to any notion of "right" and "wrong." If the data is insufficient to justify government intervention, then governments should leave the economy and markets alone.[13] Friedman, in a 1970 *New York Times* article, used Coase to argue that the single "moral" duty of a corporation was to make as much money as it could.[14] In less than a decade, under President Ronald Reagan, US policymakers went from viewing high profitability as a warning sign that a firm was growing too large and stifling competition to embracing high profits regardless of the impact on competition.[15]

---

[12] Davies, *The Happiness Industry*, 150–51.
[13] Davies, *The Happiness Industry*, 155.
[14] Davies, *The Happiness Industry*, 159.
[15] Davies, *The Happiness Industry*, 159–60.

In Australia, we have seen the consequences of this thinking when ABC Learning entered the childcare sector as a private provider. It created the problem of corporations "too big to fail" (meaning governments must bail them out when they make bad decisions) and "too big to jail" (meaning that they escape the force of the law that would apply to other businesses).

The Role of Government

Government in Australia is often conceived, especially in church circles, as though it were a standalone institution. The reality is that government as an institution is a place of struggle between different ideological positions of those elected to government and those interests in society that they represent. For any part of society to take no interest in government is, in effect, to surrender government to other parts of society that wish to use its reins to pursue their own ideological aims. If churches are serious about having an interest in the well-being of people and societies, they must take an interest in government to ensure that the policies and outcomes being pursued are consistent with the gospel vision for community and society.

Increasingly, church community service agencies are dependent on government revenue to provide services for those in need in our society. There is a risk that agencies will conform to the policy direction of the government of the day, whatever its ideology. There is fear that future funding or contracts may be placed at risk, jeopardising the ability to deliver services to people who need them along with the jobs of agency staff. Further, agencies often feel they have no grassroots base from which to conduct campaigning, reducing their belief they have any real ability to oppose a major policy direction. Agencies, as a consequence, are more likely to argue about the structure or size of a funding cut than oppose the ideology that may be driving the cut.

By working with the churches they are associated with, however, agencies could assist with and be part of broader movements seeking transformational change in society and opposing the encroachment of the neoliberal agenda for the marketisation of human services, largely delivered through for-profit businesses. At the same time, the church structures (be it assembly, synods, presbyteries, or congregations) can learn from the experience of agencies and the people that need their services.

The Importance of Government Revenue and Taxation

Government revenue is vital to a decent society. It ensures funding for human and community services that are accessible to all people regardless of their personal income, including schools, universities, hospitals, health-care clinics, mental health services, family violence services, and aged care, just to name a few. Government revenue also provides the vital funding for the bodies and institutions charged with protecting people in our community from exploitation and abuse. This includes bodies that enforce employment laws, regulatory authorities charged with protecting people in care from abuse and neglect, bodies that enforce laws against unethical marketing and predatory provision of credit, just to name a few.

As neoliberals believe in small government and the removal of regulation, because each individual should be responsible for their own well-being,[16] so they advocate for a reduction in tax revenue.[17]

Revenue is, however, only one of the four Rs that taxation serves in a society. The other three are redistribution, repricing, and representation.[18] Taxation can be used to redistribute wealth within a community, to reduce inequality and poverty, and to ensure a decent society for all its members. Repricing refers to the use of taxation to lower consumption of goods and services that have harmful effects while encouraging better options, for example, taxes on tobacco and alcohol products. A tax on pollution can cause businesses to change the way they produce goods and services to reduce pollution and encourage members of the community to use appliances that pollute less. Finally, representation refers to the role of taxation in helping to hold governments accountable to their citizens. Studies have shown that governments with higher dependence on revenue collected by taxation on their citizens are more accountable to those citizens.[19]

Rising Inequality

Rising inequality, between countries and within them, has accompanied the rise of the neoliberals and their agenda. It has proven to be a difficult conversation to have publicly. As noted by Thomas Piketty, "Whenever one speaks about the distribution of wealth, politics is never far behind, and it is difficult for anyone to escape contemporary class prejudices

---

[16] Harvey, *A Brief History of Neoliberalism*, 65.
[17] Harvey, *A Brief History of Neoliberalism*, 65.
[18] Alex Cobham, *The Tax Consensus Has Failed!* (Oxford Council on Good Governance, 2007), 2–3.
[19] Cobham, *The Tax Consensus*, 2–3.

and interests."[20] Emerging evidence also links economic inequality with decreased psychological wellbeing. Richard Wilkinson and Kate Pickett's *The Spirit Level*, through an analysis of OECD countries, found a direct link between major health and social problems to levels of income inequality.[21] People living in unequal societies were several times more likely to be in jail, be mentally ill, be obese, be murdered, and have higher infant mortality. Though a number of critiques apply to their methodology and statistical analysis, their observations point to inequality being a factor that impacts on many indicators of social well-being.

Piketty argues that within neoliberal capitalism "there is no natural, spontaneous process to prevent destabilising, inegalitarian forces from prevailing permanently."[22] Income inequality impacts on people's opportunity to move beyond or out of their social sphere. That is, the sort of family you were born into becomes a large determinant of where you end up.[23] Andrew Leigh identifies a higher participation rate, such as contacting government officials or signing petitions, in democratic processes among wealthier people. In addition, inequality can affect political outcomes by shaping our notion of the common good. "When the most affluent use different hospitals and schools, travel solely by private transport and live among those in their own income bracket, they may lose touch with the need for a strong safety net to protect the most

---

[20] Thomas Piketty, *Capital in the Twenty-First Century* (Cambridge, MA: Belknap, 2014), 4.
[21] Kate Pickett and Richard Wilkinson, *The Spirit Level* (London: Penguin Books, 2009).
[22] Piketty, *Capital in the Twenty-First Century*, 21.
[23] Andrew Leigh, *Battlers and Billionaires: The Story of Inequality in Australia* (Melbourne: Redback, 2013), 91.

disadvantaged."[24] Leigh observes the growing inequality in Australia with real wages for the bottom tenth having risen 15 percent, while wages for the top tenth have risen 59 percent. Cumulatively, the increase in inequality over the past three decades represents a $365 billion shift from the bottom 99 to the top 1 percent. His work found the richest fifty people in Australia have more wealth than the bottom two million.[25]

Tax collection has shifted under the pressures of tax competition between governments for the benefit of the very wealthy, with the effect of worsening inequality within countries. The tax situation of the world's very wealthy is improving as a result of tax competition. Tax collection on corporations has fallen in comparison to tax collection on labour and spending, which has demonstrably increased inequality. Research by the Australia Institute found the Howard and Rudd governments had transferred large sums of public money to the wealthy in the form of a tax cut. Australia's highest income earners got one of the largest tax cuts in the developed world in the past decade—surpassing the unfunded tax cuts of the US George W. Bush administration. In 2000, upper-middle income earners were taxed at an effective tax rate of 38.3 percent, which dropped to 31.7 percent in 2010.[26] Of the $169 billion in tax cuts given out in between 2006 and 2013, $71 billion went to the highest 10 percent of income

---

[24] Leigh, *Battlers and Billionaires*, 89.
[25] Andrew Leigh, "Gap Between Haves and Have Nots Must Be Narrowed," *The Australian*, 21 April 2014.
[26] George Megalogenis, "How Our Rich Were Given Some of the World's Biggest Tax Cuts," *The Australian*, 21 September 2011.

earners. The top 10 percent of income earners got more than the bottom 80 percent.[27]

A report on inequality by Australia21, the Australian National University, and the Australia Institute noted that the wealthiest 20 percent of households in Australia now account for 61 percent of total household net worth, whereas the poorest 20 percent account for just 1 percent of the total. In recent decades, the income share of the top 1 percent has doubled, and the wealth share of the top 0.001 percent has more than tripled.[28]

Australians want a more equal society and support people being paid at a more equal rate. They also support the government using tax to redistribute wealth. A survey of Australian attitudes on wealth inequality and taxation found that Australians dramatically underestimate the degree of wealth inequality within their society and favour a society becoming more equal in terms of wealth distribution.[29] This desire to live in a more equal society is relatively stable across political ideologies. By strong majorities, all political groups least preferred living in a country with Australia's current level of wealth inequality. Despite Australians supporting a more equal wealth distribution and a progressive taxation, they have not forged strong links between the two issues. Respondents also supported government adopting policies that would promote wealth equality in Australia.[30]

---

[27] Matt Grudnoff, "Tax Cuts That Broke the Budget," *Policy Brief*, no. 52 (2013): 1.

[28] Bob Douglas et al., *Australia Fair? What to Do about Growing Inequality in Australia* (Canberra: Australia21, 2014), 8.

[29] David Neale, Mike Norton, and Dan Ariely, *Australian Attitudes Towards Wealth Inequality and Progressive Taxation* (ACTU, 2011), 7.

[30] Neale, Norton, and Ariely, *Australian Attitudes*, 17.

This suggests the majority of Australians would support the churches in seeking a more egalitarian society, which is more in line with the vision of the Gospels and the way the early followers of Jesus lived as noted in the book of Acts.

Privatisation and Marketisation of Human Services

Instead of acknowledging that some human services are best provided by government, the neoliberal trend is to view government as the provider of last resort for human and community services. There are also human service areas where for-profit providers are the worst option for government to pursue, based on public interest and the common good.

The trend of privatisation and marketisation is likely to pose an ongoing threat for UnitingCare/Uniting community service agencies, if the trends seen in places like the United Kingdom are replicated in Australia. Though government services are tendered out to not-for-profit providers, this is only a way station towards the ultimate goal of full marketisation, where for-profits are able to move in and gain the delivery of the bulk of the services. This matters because of the harm it does not only to the people needing the service but also to the people working to deliver the service and the broader society.

Human services should be assessed by their overall benefit to society. For example, a reduction in regulation of disability service providers may result in reduced administration costs for such providers. But if this comes at the cost of a net increase in the prevalence of abuse and neglect of people with disabilities accessing the services, then there is a net loss to the type of society Australia is. Similarly, if turning the provision of a human service into a more competitive market drives up the illegal exploitation of people working in that sector, there may be a benefit to people accessing the service (through reduced costs) and to government (through lower funding being needed). Illegal exploitation, however, has a negative impact on society as a whole. The privatisation of human services, or turning them into markets when they are not natural markets, needs to be considered from the perspective not only of individual services competing in the new system but also of the trends driving the changes and whether those trends benefit the society and the people using the service.

Evidence from behavioural science suggests that if we use money to motivate people it will drive behaviours that are selfish and self-reliant.[31] Does society benefit when our human service providers become more selfish and self-reliant as a result of privatisation and marketisation? If this reduces the sharing of best practice in the delivery of the service, then society and the users of the service will be worse off (although the propagation of best practice might happen when staff move between services). For example, UnitingCare agencies report that the roll-out of the National Disability Insurance Scheme market model is likely to result in agencies being less cooperative and less likely to share innovations as they compete for every person accessing their services.[32] Similarly, UnitingCare housing agencies report that increased market competition between providers can harm the culture of cooperation and cross-referral between agencies. This impacts

---

[31] Dan Ariely, *Predictably Irrational* (London: Harper, 2009), 74–75.
[32] UnitingCare Australia, "Submission to the Productivity Commission Inquiry into Introducing Competition and Informed User Choice into Human Services," 25 July 2016, 8.

the options that are available to people needing the housing services.³³

As noted by an employee of a UnitingCare agency:

> Having delivered services under DSS Employment contracts for 10 years, we can attest that the competitive market has significantly reduced collaboration and partnership models due to the competitive star rating system, we have been driven to create efficiencies and this has meant poorer outcomes for clients because we have had to have higher caseloads, are unable to add work outside of the contract and the measures do not capture or reward the additional outcomes for clients.³⁴

Creating markets in human services can also cause perverse behaviour in people using the services. A child day care centre introduced a fine for parents who arrived late to pick up their children as a market signal to get the parents to pick the children up on time. It had the opposite effect. Before the fine, as part of the social contract, if a parent was late he or she would feel guilty about it, and the guilt often encouraged greater attention to picking up the child on time. Once the fine was imposed, the parents applied the market norm and saw the day care centre as offering additional care at the cost of the fine. Late pick-ups increased, which was the opposite effect of what the centre had wanted. Even after the fine was removed, the parents continued to be more likely to pick their children up late. In fact, late pick-ups increased as both the social contract and the market signal were removed.³⁵

---

[33] UnitingCare Australia, "Submission," 9.
[34] UnitingCare Australia, "Submission," 13.
[35] Ariely, *Predictably Irrational*, 76–77; Michael Sandel, *What Money Can't Buy: The Moral Limits of Markets* (London: Penguin, 2013).

Privatising or marketising human and community services carries the following risks:

1. A reduction in the quality of the service for those that need to use the service.
2. Increased exploitation of the workforce and risk of illegal exploitation of the workforce. For example, in the United Kingdom, privately employed home care staff are being paid less because they are not paid for the travelling time between appointments. In 2009 and 2010, there was an increase in the number of fifteen- and thirty-minute appointments assigned by employers, and a decrease in sixty-minute appointments, increasing the amount of unpaid transit time employees needed to spend between appointments.[36]
3. Government revenue being stolen through fraud or being gamed by providers that provide a substandard service. In many human service areas there will be people who cannot afford to pay for the service they need, and thus many service providers will ultimately receive the payment from the government, be it by direct payment from government or though the government providing the funding to the person needing the service. Creating a sustainable human services sector is paramount when programs are addressing long-term, multilayered, and/or intergenerational disadvantage, or in cases where positive outcomes for children and young people in out-of-home care or adults with disabilities in supported accommodation

---

[36] Zoe Williams, "The Shadow State: A Report about Outsourcing of Public Services" (Social Enterprise UK, 2012), 9, http://www.huckfield.com/wp-content/uploads/2013/01/12-SEUK-Shadow-State-Dec1.pdf.

require long-term commitment to secure stable placement and attachment.[37]

4. Eroding the quality of the workforce in the sector, be it through lowering of what gets paid for the service, through workloads that prohibit time for professional development, or through creating an environment of job insecurity so that people are not attracted to work in the sector. Lower wages and greater job insecurity drive up staff turnover in services, which can have significant impacts on the quality of care users of the service receive. For example, the client now needs to retell his or her case history multiple times due to high staff turnover.

5. Privatisation or marketisation could result in some people being excluded from accessing a service they need. This can happen when what the government is willing to contract the service out for is too low for the providers to provide the service. Or it can happen because providers decide to "redline" certain groups of people that need the service to maximise profit, even if the government is providing sufficient funding for the service. It can also happen when existing providers cross-subsidise services to higher-cost (higher-need) people from lower-cost people, and then new providers are able to enter the market and cherry-pick the lower-cost people using the service, destroying the cross-subsidising model of the existing providers. In the United Kingdom, this type of behaviour by private service providers has earned the nickname "creaming and parking": low-cost people using the service

---

[37] Sally Cowling and Romola Hollywood, *Submission to Productivity Commission Inquiry into the Contribution of the Not-for-Profit Sector* (Sydney: UnitingCare Children, Young People and Families, 2009), 4.

get support while the rest get parked (provided with no real service).[38]
6. Greater privatisation or marketisation can result in system fragmentation, making it harder for people who have complex needs to have those needs met. Competition between service providers can work against a joined-up approach to complex user needs.
7. Resources can be wasted in order to have a "real market." For a real market to exist, all users must at all times have the option of choice. For example, if people living in a particular town are to have a market for hospital services, that means there must be at least two accessible hospitals and both must have spare capacity at all times. If one hospital is full at any given time, then the remaining users will have no choice but to use the other hospital. To maintain a free market there will need to be redundant capacity at all times in both hospitals, when one hospital which has effective regulatory oversight to ensure its quality would have been better. Marketisation also means resources that could have been used for service delivery are instead used for marketing to attract users.

UnitingCare Australia has reported that their child and family services now need to employ more people on a casual basis to deliver services. Casual employment offers less stability for the employed and has the potential to impact on the qualification of the employee and access to support. Additionally, UnitingCare agencies report that greater use

---

[38] See, for example, Richard Johnson, "The Work Programme's Only Success Is at 'Creaming and Parking'," *The Guardian*, 21 February, 2013, https://www.theguardian.com/commentisfree/2013/feb/20/work-programme-success-creaming-parking.

of casual employees can mean a lack of continuity in care for those receiving the service. Continuity is often a key preference.[39]

The marketisation of human services also assumes that the people needing the service are able to make informed decisions on what service will be best for them and their needs. The reality is that, in some cases, the circumstances will prohibit a person needing the service from shopping around. For example, a person with a serious injury that needs immediate medical treatment would be unlikely to shop around for the best value emergency department if emergency departments at hospitals were turned into a market.

There are more mundane examples of market failure. In the energy market (an essential need for people) the St Vincent de Paul Society has concluded that "[w]e have an energy retail market that ensures customers are paying over the odds for an essential service unless they annually dedicate time to compare energy plans and switch plan or retailer."[40] At the same time, they found that people in the energy market are increasingly disengaging from participation in the market.[41] The same report, quoting the Australian Energy Market Commission, found that people within particular demographics were less likely to participate in the energy market and therefore would pay more for their energy by remaining on the standing (default) offers:

---

[39] UnitingCare Australia, "Submission," 8.

[40] Gavin Dufty and May Mauseth Johnston, "The National Energy Market – Still Winging It: Observations from the Vinnies' Tariff-Tracking Project" (St Vincent de Paul Society and Alviss Consulting, 2015), 6, https://www.vinnies.org.au/icms_docs/228265_National_Energy_Market_-_Still_Winging_It.pdf.

[41] Dufty and Johnston, "The National Energy Market," 5, 29–30.

> [C]ustomers on standing offers are more likely to be customers who are older or living in regional areas. In Melbourne and Sydney, higher income areas are more likely to have a high proportion of customers on standing offers. The reverse applies in many regional areas where lower income areas are more likely to have customers on standing offers.[42]

Many people needing a service will be forced to rely on less than optimal assessment information, the experience of family and friends, for example, to decide on a human service in a market. Such a method is hardly sufficiently scientific and rigorous to determine the best service for the user's need, but it may be the only one that the person needing the service can realistically undertake.

There is a real danger that increased marketisation of human services will result in high-quality community and volunteer services being crowded out, as has been the experience in the United Kingdom.[43] Market failure can lead to excessive prices for consumers, inadequate supply of required services, low-quality services, and exploitation of consumers, particularly vulnerable consumers. Any moves to increase competition for human services must be accompanied by strong regulation to protect consumer interests. The regulatory structures and an associated regulatory body also need to be vigilant in identifying market failure and proposing a remedy for such failure.

Social losses can also result from the marketisation of human services. For example, a "meals on wheels" service could be understood as providing a regular nutritious meal to a diverse range of regular customers. The driving objective

---
[42] Dufty and Johnston, "The National Energy Market," 37.
[43] Williams, "The Shadow State," 5.

for market competition would then be to reduce the unit cost of meals delivered and to improve efficiency of delivery so that more meals are delivered per hour. Such an approach would largely miss the added benefit of meals on wheels—providing a security and safety check through a regular visit for many people who are living alone. The service may constitute the only human interaction a person receives in a day or even in a week. The short chat between the person delivering the meal and the person receiving the meal can be more important than the caloric value of the particular meal. Yet, an efficiency focus on meal delivery could see this crucial function curtailed or even eliminated. This would dramatically reduce the total quality and effectiveness of the whole service by increasing the perceived efficiency of one aspect of the service.

Case Study—The Marketisation of the Vocational, Education, and Training Sector

The recent changes in the Vocational Education, and Training (VET) sector in Australia show the disastrous outcomes that can result for people accessing services and government expenditure when poorly regulated and designed markets are rushed through and imposed on the community. The federal government has acknowledged that the rapid marketisation of the VET sector in 2012 "did not contain sufficient safeguards for students or regulatory powers for the department, instead providing incentives and rewards for unethical behaviour."[44]

---

[44] Australian Government, "Redesigning VET FEE-HELP. Discussion Paper," 5, https://docs.education.gov.au/system/files/doc/other/redesigning_vet _fee-help_-_discussion_paper_0_0.pdf.

There was a massive increase in students accessing the VET FEE-HELP scheme, from 55,000 in 2012 to more than 272,000 in 2015, and more than one hundred new private Registered Training Organisations (RTOs) moved in for a feeding frenzy on government funding. The government has acknowledged that some of this was fuelled by unethical marketing practices of VET providers targeting disadvantaged groups. The unethical marketing practices included offering inducements such as iPads, cash, and vouchers to prospective students to enrol in a course and request VET FEE-HELP:

> These behaviours specifically targeted vulnerable people through cold calling or door knocking neighbourhoods of low socio-economic status. Those targeted were signed up to a course which they may not have the academic capability to complete and may not understand that the loan needed repaying.[45]

This resulted in a massive cost to government revenue, with VET FEE-HELP payments from government to VET providers increasing from $325 million in 2012 to $2.9 billion in 2015.[46] As shown in table 1, an alarming proportion of the funding has been wasted. While, in theory, the government should be able to recover the money from the defrauded students, it acknowledges that many may never earn a high enough income to be compelled to repay the VET FEE-HELP debt (unless the government changes the income threshold at which the student must start to repay the loan). Part of the waste that has been generated through the poorly regulated VET market is due to inflated course costs, with students unaware of the true costs of delivering courses. Course tuition

---

[45] Australian Government, "Redesigning VET FEE-HELP," 14.
[46] Australian Government, "Redesigning VET FEE-HELP," 15.

fees increased from an average of $4,000 in 2009 to $14,000 in 2015.[47] Some unethical providers fraudulently marketed their courses as being free.[48] The government has concluded that the false perception that courses are free means "the costs of courses with access to VET FEE-HELP now bears little relationship to the true (efficient) cost of delivery."[49]

Table 1. Selected Providers of VET in 2014[50]

Provider	Amount received from VET FEE-HELP ($ millions)	Number of VET FEE-HELP students enrolled in 2014	Number of students that graduated	Cost to VET FEE-HELP per graduation ($)
Evocca College	$250.2	26,848	1,053	$237,592
AIPE	$110.0	8,814	117	$939,805
Study Group	$101.7	13,715	470	$216,414
Unique	$76.8	2,824	172	$446,318
Cornerstone Investments	$46.1	4,251	2	$23,068,008
College of Creative Design and the Arts	$35.5	3,530	30	$1,182,456

The government reported that in 2014 the completion rates of courses running for two years was only 22 percent, down from 26 percent in 2013.[51] For Indigenous students, completion rates in 2014 were only 12.6 percent, and across all students

---

[47] Australian Government, "Redesigning VET FEE-HELP," 16.
[48] Australian Government, "Redesigning VET FEE-HELP," 17.
[49] Australian Government, "Redesigning VET FEE-HELP," 17.
[50] Senate Education and Employment Committee, Question on Notice Number SQ15-000668, https://www.aph.gov.au/~/media/Committees/eet_ctte/estimates/supp_1516/Education/Answers/SQ15-000668.pdf.
[51] Australian Government, "Redesigning VET FEE-HELP," 19.

the completion rate for online courses (which were those most likely to be scams) was only 7 percent.[52] As noted by the government:

> VET FEE-HELP can also incentivize providers to offer training which attracts the highest subsidy, benefit or profit, at the lowest cost. Low cost strategies include delivering training online which reduces costs associated with teaching staff, rent and equipment needed for certain courses.[53]

By comparison, the estimated completion rate for VET FEE-HELP supported students commencing in 2013 and studying diploma level and above was 42.2 percent.[54]

Table 2 shows the difference in the costs of courses based on what the NSW government paid under the Smart and Skilled initiative in 2013 and what the average tuition fee is for the same course when delivered by a VET provider under the VET FEE-HELP scheme. As noted by the government:

> These differences reflect a substantial market failure, that providers are able to extract margins that are substantially higher, likely due to a serious information asymmetry, and particularly poor consumer information or access to it.[55]

---

[52] Australian Government, "Redesigning VET FEE-HELP," 19.
[53] Australian Government, "Redesigning VET FEE-HELP," 22.
[54] Australian Government, "Redesigning VET FEE-HELP," 19.
[55] Australian Government, "Redesigning VET FEE-HELP," 18.

Table 2. Average VET FEE-HELP Tuition Fees versus Qualification Price Set under NSW Government Smart and Skilled[56]

Course	Average tuition fee per full time VET FEE-HELP student	NSW Smart and Skilled Qualification Price
Diploma of Salon Management	$32,941	$6,330
Diploma of Project Management	$29,065	$6,490
Diploma of Marketing	$28,596	$5,800
Diploma of Events	$14,567	$8,980
Diploma of Accounting	$13,659	$6,570

The failure of regulation in the expansion of markets in the VET sector has had the greatest impact on disadvantaged groups, as demonstrated in table 3, with students of Indigenous background and those from low socio-economic backgrounds paying more for VET courses than other students. As the government concludes, "These figures are extremely troubling, both for their impact on disadvantaged Australians and the unavoidable conclusion that this program has seen them taken advantage of by unscrupulous and unethical practices."[57]

---

[56] Australian Government, "Redesigning VET FEE-HELP," 17.
[57] Australian Government, "Redesigning VET FEE-HELP," 19.

Table 3. *2015 VET FEE-HELP Mean Tuition Fee by Student Demographics and Mode of Delivery*[58]

Demographic	Face-to-face	Online	Mixed-mode	Mean annual tuition fee
Indigenous	$20,448	$19,875	$18,007	$19,977
Non-Indigenous	$12,972	$16,515	$12,042	$14,328
Low SES (Quintile 1)	$15,153	$18,127	$12,970	$16,193
High SES (Quintile 5)	$11,555	$15,114	$11,151	$12,835

The Uniting Church's Position and Role in Creating a Better Society

The Uniting Church's vision for the world is one "marked by regard for the common good." We believe that "[i]ndividualism, competition and greed deny human flourishing because the fullness of our humanity is not found in wealth but in relationship with each other and the world around us."[59] With the significant role that UnitingCare/Uniting plays in delivering community services and their contact with the most vulnerable in our society, the Uniting Church is in a strong position to influence the future direction of our society. But this requires that both the congregational part of the church and the community service agencies unite in such a mission. Such collaboration already exists to a degree, but a more intentional

---

[58] Australian Government, "Redesigning VET FEE-HELP," 18.
[59] Elenie Poulos, *An Economy of Life: Reimagining Human Progress for a Flourishing World* (Sydney: Uniting Church in Australia, 2009), 13.

effort would be needed from both parts of the church if the Uniting Church's full potential in this space is to be realised.

The Uniting Church's voice is often heard by governments, and the church's opinion is sought on many economic and social issues due to the technical expertise that exists within the church. This provides a base on which to build. Of course, any attempt to change society so that it provides a decent life for all its members, where government helps facilitate all people to reach their full potential, and where government restrains greedy people and corporations from harming vulnerable people, will require much more than the Uniting Church in Australia alone. But the Uniting Church in Australia has a demonstrated record of working ecumenically, with all faiths, and with other community groups and unions.

The Uniting Church is seen as credible and acting with integrity on social issues. For example, it has campaigned in support of changes to antidiscrimination laws to reduce religious exemptions which have, in the past, granted religious bodies wide-ranging powers to discriminate even on characteristics such as race and disability. While far from perfect, it has been an early mover in addressing issues of child sexual abuse within the church. Such actions mean that the Uniting Church has built social capital to speak on social and economic matters.

But barriers remain to the Uniting Church reaching its full potential in influencing society to better reflect the gospel. The current governance structure of non-hierarchical interrelated councils has often led to a culture of individualism, both with the staff working for the church and working within its community service agencies. This, in turn, has worked against developing a common and consistent narrative of the Uniting Church's vision for a better society. For example, the Uniting

Church's fund-raising activities often promote a message that private charity is the pathway to deliver a better society, while the social justice arms of the church argue that structures, laws, regulation, and their enforcement need to change if a just society and just world are to be possible. These are two different ways of telling the story or narrative about how change is brought about. There is increasing understanding among communication specialists and social scientists that if a body or a movement wishes to bring about deeper social change then a consistent narrative is vital.[60]

Collaboration is needed to ensure the church's resources are concentrated and so able to build enough momentum to make change possible or likely. Across the churches, efforts towards change are often scattered across far too many issues to make change likely. The ability of an organisation to influence change is often only when those efforts are coordinated and strategically focused.

The Uniting Church in Australia is also often hampered by a culture of being its own worst critic. This needs to be turned around. The different parts of the church need to support each other. This requires alignment on an agreed vision, with common, achievable goals that all parts of the church are striving for. Theologians within the Uniting Church in Australia, through their teaching, research, and writing, play a vital role in unpacking and overcoming the neoliberal agenda and offering an alternative vision for society from out

---

[60] See, for example, George Lakoff, *Don't Think of an Elephant* (White River Junction, VT: Chelsea Green Publishing, 2004); Anat Shenker-Osario, *Don't Buy It: The Trouble with Talking Nonsense about the Economy* (New York: Public Affairs, 2012); and Tom Holmes, Elena Blackmore, Richard Dawkins, and Tom Wakeford, *The Common Cause Handbook* (London: Public Interest Research Centre, 2012).

of our Christian faith. The Uniting Church is well placed to provide a significant contribution to building a decent society more aligned to our faith, but it remains to be seen if we can unite our efforts for that outcome.

www.ingramcontent.com/pod-product-compliance
Lightning Source LLC
Chambersburg PA
CBHW011316080526
44588CB00020B/2728